The Embroiderer's Story

Early eighteenth-century pastoral picture in wools highlighted with silks

The Embroiderer's Story
Needlework from the Renaissance to the Present Day

Thomasina Beck

David & Charles

For Christopher

Page 1
Mid-seventeenth-century panel of a lute player in laidwork

Page 3
'Jacob wrestling with an Angel', detail from a valance, 1594

Opposite
Border of a mid-seventeenth-century raised work mirror frame

A DAVID & CHARLES BOOK

Copyright © Thomasina Beck 1995

First published 1995

A catalogue record for this book is available from the British Library.

ISBN 0 7153 0238 8

Typeset by ABM Typographics, Hull
and printed in Italy by Lego SpA
for David & Charles
Brunel House Newton Abbott Devon

Contents

O FOR a heart to praise my God,
  A heart from guilt set free,
A heart that's sprinkled with the blood
  So freely shed for me !

A heart resign'd, submissive meek,
  Our great Redeemer's throne.
Where only Christ is heard to speak,
  Where Jesus reigns alone.

A humble lowly contrite heart,
  Believing, true and clean;
Which neither life nor death can part
  From him that dwells within.

Thy nature, gracious Lord, impart,
  Come quickly from above;
Write thy new name upon my heart,
  Thy new, best name of love !

Laura Nancy Dunn

Aged fourteen

Years

Taught by her Mother

Introduction

In 1657 a twelve-year-old girl named Hannah Smith placed a note in one of the drawers of the embroidered cabinet she had completed the previous year. The note tells of the two years she spent in Oxford working on the project and of the exciting moment when the embroidered panels were sent away to London to be mounted on the cabinet. She tells us she wrote the note in order to record her satisfaction and sense of achievement on completing such a beautiful piece of work, lest at some later time in her life she might have forgotten about it.

Many of Hannah's contemporaries made similar cabinets, some of them even more intricate in stitchery and design. They testify to the exceptional technical expertise of the period, but they tell us little, or nothing, about the makers and the part embroidery played in their lives. Hannah's note makes her cabinet unique because it reveals a rare glimpse of an individual embroiderer at work in the middle of the seventeenth century. She obligingly tells us how long the embroidery took (a question that particularly intrigues enthusiasts of later generations) but, more importantly, she expresses feelings that we as embroiderers can relate to at once, as we too have experienced the same pleasure and satisfaction when a special project is completed, and we too want it to be valued. She ends her note telling us that it was written not only for her benefit, but for 'those that shall enquire about it'. This last

Opposite *Early Victorian sampler, one of a pair worked in coloured silks by Laura Nancy Dunn and her younger sister Ann Lydia with help and encouragement from their mother. Both girls recorded the family pet, traditionally a popular subject in needlework (see pages 19, 84 and 150). Laura's spirited portrait of the dog is matched in charm by Ann's vignette of the two girls stroking him. Suggestions for adapting the motifs on their samplers for use today are shown on page 10*

Hannah Smith began embroidering the panels of her cabinet in 1654 when she was nine. She worked the biblical scenes on the doors (see page 50) mainly in tent stitch in silks, and the lion and leopard on the lid in raised work on satin

phrase seemed to me a direct invitation to find out more about Hannah and her contemporaries in order to answer some of the questions posed by their work. Where did they find the designs and who drew out the patterns for them? Why, for example, did they so often choose biblical subjects to ornament the cabinets and pictures they made? Did they have guidance with the complex stitches, and if so from whom? Histories, biographies, novels, diaries and poems provided some of the answers, and I began piecing snippets of information together, as one might a collage, hoping thereby to build up a picture of what it was like to be an embroiderer at that time. Fascination with the pattern sources and virtuoso stitchery inevitably led me back into the Elizabethan age, and then on into the eighteenth century to see how they had evolved. Research into the elusive figure of the embroiderer became addictive, and I determined to build up not one, but a series of pictures.

'Embroidery is essentially a personal art', wrote Walter Crane (in 1899 in the preface to *Embroidery or the Craft of the Needle*), and this book is essentially about the people – the men, women and children – who found, and still find, pleasure in stitchery. It is concerned mainly with domestic needlework, and makes no pretence at being a formal history. I have limited the scope to Britain, and my aim, whenever possible, is to let the embroiderers tell the story in their own words, and then fill in the background to their lives, describing the tools, materials, patterns and

A lion similar to Hannah Smith's appears on the title page of A Book of Beast. . . *(1630), depicting Orpheus charming the beasts. Book illustrations provided recurrent motifs for embroidery and have remained a rich source of inspiration as Patricia Lois Sales' Alice found it very difficult to manage her flamingo, 1993, (opposite) shows. Based on Tenniel's illustrations in* Alice in Wonderland, *the motifs are machine embroidered and applied to a space-dyed ground, finished with hand stitching and padding*

books that were available to them, and showing how their work was influenced by the style of their period, by changing social and religious factors, and by trade, travel and commerce. If the emphasis appears to be principally on 'the great who live profusely, the rich who live plentifully, and the middle class who live well' – the top three of the classes listed by Defoe in Britain in 1709 – this is because embroidering for pleasure remained the privilege of those classes until the close of the eighteenth century.

I have chosen to begin with the Elizabethan age, not only because of the wealth of dress and furnishing embroideries that survive, but because the embroiderers themselves provide vital evidence which is backed up by information in wills, inventories and portraits. The secular embroideries so tantalisingly described in medieval documents were mainly professional work, of which little remains, and evidence concerning domestic embroiderers is so fragmentary that they remain shadowy figures.

The Elizabethans had no notion of the kits, sophisticated sewing machines and photocopiers that have made such an impact on twentieth-century embroidery, but the ultra-sharp scissors and needles developed in their day had just as revolutionary an effect on their work. They experienced the same pleasure as we do in handling fine tools and beautiful materials, the same excitement in finding the perfect motif to start a project and the same satisfaction in engrossing themselves in it, but, conversely, their concept of time was very different from ours. In many households, hours each day were devoted to needlework. To 'work' meant to do needlework and this use of the word remained common until late in the nineteenth century.

On 19 December 1798 Lady Eleanor Butler and Sarah Ponsonby (generally known as 'the Ladies of Llangollen') were busy 'Reading, working'. Eleanor, Sarah tells us, 'finished the white satin letter case with the cyphers in gold, with a border of shades of pale blue and gold, the quilting white silk, the whole lined and bound in pale blue'. The letter case has not survived, but visitors to Plas Newydd, their romantically gothicised retreat in Wales, can still see Sarah's work-bag embroidered with a delicate spray of flowers – a faded relic, but one which speaks eloquently of happy, companionable days, and encapsulates a lost lifestyle. As Averil Colby noted in her book on

Pincushions (1975), 'We can penetrate into the past more easily through the small things that people have loved than through the great.' Needlework can evoke fragments of individual lives in a uniquely moving way, as children's samplers often bear witness.

Samplers play an important role in this story as they often pinpoint changing styles and attitudes to embroidery more accurately than general 'pigeonhole' terms such as 'Regency' or 'Victorian', which suggest a misleadingly abrupt change of style between one period and another. Until the twentieth century, sampler making was taken for granted as the normal way to get started in needlework. They were originally intended as a storehouse of ideas for future projects, and, as Belinda Downes' illustrations show, the inventive patterns and beguiling motifs can still provide all sorts of suggestions for contemporary designs.

The embroiderers of the past had professionals to help them with pattern drawing, but they also made extensive use of printed sources of all kinds, some recent, others dating back a century or more. Many of the woodcuts, engravings and book illustrations that appealed to them are reproduced here in the hope that they may inspire another generation of embroiderers who will interpret them in their own way.

Paddy Killer's pictures of tools and chapter headings were inspired by the needlework of the period, and by contemporary portraits, engravings, drawings and fashion plates – except the last in which she depicts herself. Each one reflects a method popular at the time: Elizabethan blackwork, Stuart raised work, Georgian canvaswork, Regency whitework, Victorian Art Embroidery and twentieth-century machine embroidery.

The pet dogs, flower garlands, trees and butterflies worked by the Dunn sisters (see page 6) provide Belinda Downes with new ideas for sampler and picture making

The Elizabethan Embroiderer

They must be careful, diligent and wise,
In Needleworkes that beare away the Prise.
William Barley, 1596

In the New Year of 1600, Arabella Stuart, grand-daughter of Bess of Hardwick, sent Queen Elizabeth a present of her own making. The Elizabethans delighted in giving and receiving presents, and the New Year was a favourite time to exchange them. Arabella's gift was a 'scarf or head veil of lawn cutwork flourished with silver and silk of sundry colours', which would have taken many hours and great skill to embroider.

She would have begun by cutting out holes in the material to form a pattern. While cutwork is normally worked on firm white linen with matching linen thread, Arabella chose fine lawn, which would have made over-sewing the edges of the holes and filling them with cobweb-fine patterns exceptionally fiddly. Well aware of Queen Elizabeth's enthusiasm for fine needlework, Arabella had opted for this difficult technique in the hope that her scarf would catch the Queen's eye. But in 1600 the array of embroidered gifts was particularly spectacular, with over sixty items including gowns, doublets, pillow covers, cloaks, caps and no less than four other scarves vying for her attention. Arabella must have been relieved to hear that hers had been noticed and that the

A lady, said to be Arabella Stuart, wearing a jacket trimmed with cutwork. Portrait attributed to Marcus Gheeraerts, c.1605

Cutwork patterns from Sibmacher's Modelbuch *(1597)*

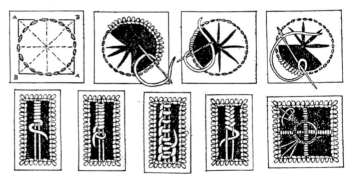

The refined effect of cutwork is shown on both the jacket and the table-

cover in this portrait of Frances, Countess of Essex. British School, c.1605

Cutting squares and circles, securing the edges with buttonhole or overcast stitches, and then filling

the space with patterns worked over bars explained in Embroidery *(September 1933)*

Queen had 'taken an especial liking' to it, and even more gratified to receive a message that Her Majesty 'would be glad to know how she did it'. Queen Elizabeth speaks here not as a sovereign, but as one embroiderer to another, expressing admiration for Arabella's originality and faultless technique, and a possible interest in trying out something similar herself.

The little phrase 'to know how she did it' has echoes in every century, and is still heard whenever embroiderers meet to admire inventive stitchery. It takes us straight into the world of the Elizabethan embroiderer, devising increasingly intricate patterns and stitches that dazzle us today when we study the impressive portraits of the age or visit a great house like Hardwick Hall, with its echoes of Bess and her grand-daughter.

Enthusiasm for embroidery was then unparalleled; it ornamented every conceivable item of dress or furnishings, from a toothcloth bordered in blackwork (made by Queen Elizabeth's laundress before the advent of toothbrushes), to hangings bright with birds, flowers and lovers in an arbour. It was admired as an art, and seen as an

uniquely satisfying way of showing off taste and wealth.

Skill at needlework was considered an essential accomplishment, enabling any gentlewoman who acquired it to transform her home and wardrobe, and to follow the fashion for lavish display. Status and social aggrandisement were all-important and the acquisition of wealth and its conspicuous spending were admired and emulated. A more stable government, developing industries and expanding trade overseas brought prosperity, and the newly rich bought land and built impressive houses in towns and in the countryside. A competitive spirit was in the air, and fortunes were spent on dress, and on making the home more luxurious than ever before. 'Twere good you turned four or five acres of your best land into two or three trunks of apparel', suggests one of the characters in Ben Jonson's *Every Man in his Humour* (1601), and many aspiring courtiers followed his advice, and exceeded it, running up huge debts to tailors, mercers and embroiderers. Elaborate outfits for men and women, richly decorated with stylish and idiosyncratic motifs revealed 'the fancy of him that weareth it', while furnishings were

Queen Elizabeth led the fashion for strikingly embroidered dress. In this portrait the rich embroidery of gold roses, honeysuckle and birds heightens the contrast with the delicate cutwork ruff and diaphanous head veil. British School, c.1600

A lady, with her pet dog, wearing a stomacher and sleeves idiosyncratically embroidered with a unicorn and oriental figures together with roses, borage and insects. British School, c.1590

equally imaginative, their textures, colours and patterns bringing warmth, gaiety and comfort to the interior – there was every possible incentive to excel in the art.

In great houses, in the manor houses of the gentry and homes of prosperous city merchants and farmers, girls were taught to stitch from earliest childhood. 'This worke', wrote William Barley in 1596 in his *Booke of Curious and Strange Inventions,*

> Beseemeth Queens of great renown
> And noble ladies of a high degree,
> Yet not exempt for Maids of any Towne
> For all may learn that thereto willing be.

His book, intended for 'the Profit and Delight of the Gentlewomen of England', contained a variety of cutwork patterns, as needlework was 'not only requisite, but also in great request among the Gentry'. He pokes fun at 'maidens but of base degree' who saw it as a way of moving up the social ladder and becoming 'esteemed among the noblest sort'.

The 'Queens of great renown' included Katherine of Aragon (who embroidered shirts for Henry VIII), Anne Boleyn and Queen Elizabeth. As a child the young princess made three bookbindings as New Year gifts, one for her father and two for her step-mother Katherine Parr. Embroidered in silver and red and blue threads, with heart's-ease and initials intertwined, they show just how skilled an eleven-year-old could be, and the contents are equally impressive, for here the erudite princess shows off her knowledge of French and Latin in her translations of devotional texts, written in her own clear hand. The growing awareness of the importance of education for women owed much to her example, and needlework was

Above *Bookbinding,* How We Ought to Know God *worked in 1545 by Princess Elizabeth*

Late sixteenth-century valance depicting the education of Princess Elizabeth

Intricate patterning in coloured silks and silvergilt thread on a late sixteenth-century cover

Strawberry, rose and columbine from Turner's New Herball, *1551-68*

Below *Coiling stem and diaper patterns adapted from a late Elizabethan cushion and cover*

considered an indispensable part of any properly brought up girl's education. Writing in 1561, the kindly schoolmaster Richard Mulcaster expressed the view that all girls should learn 'reading, writing, music, sight singing, skill in needlework and housewifery', and then, depending on their ability and position in society, speak 'learned languages as well as modern tongues' and draw 'to beautify their needlework'.

Such a curriculum, and especially the last recommendation, is vividly recalled in a description of childhood written by Grace Sherrington, who was born in 1552. She was the second daughter of Sir Henry Sherrington of Lacock Abbey in Wiltshire, and late in her life she filled a black bound volume with reminiscences of her youth at Lacock, and then of her married years at Apethorpe near Northampton. Originally a convent, and then purchased from the crown in 1540, Lacock had been gradually transformed into a manor house. In Sir Henry's day its interior was lavishly decorated with tapestries and embroidered furnishings, all meticulously described in an inventory of 1575.

Like most girls of her time Grace was educated at home, where she had the good fortune to be brought up by Mistress Hamblyn, a poor relation of the family, who combined firmness with good humour and sense. Grace 'delighted so much in her companye that she would sit by her all day in her chamber, and by good will never go from her, embracing allways her rebukes and reproofs'. Together they would study the Bible, sing psalms and pore over Doctor William Turner's recently published *New Herball* with its pictures of plants and advice on their properties. Mistress Hamblyn was an expert herbalist, 'with good knowledge in physick'. She saw to it that her pupil was never idle; she made her practise writing – not just handwriting, but business letters – and taught her to keep accounts, skills which would prove invaluable when Grace came to manage her own household.

Mistress Hamblyn was 'an excellent workwoman in all kinds of needlework, and most curiously she would perform it'. 'Curious' at that time meant 'neatly detailed' and 'elegant' rather than odd or peculiar, so when she set Grace 'to some curious work', we can imagine her first demonstrating a stitch, and then seeing her pupil practise till she could work it perfectly. They would begin with the basic stitches of plain sewing – running and back stitch for example – and only when Grace could hem and seam nicely would her governess have instructed her in the more decorative stitches. Grace gained a taste for embroidery that lasted all her life, and she was to pass on to her own daughter all that she had learned from Mistress Hamblyn.

Grace was married at sixteen to Sir Antony Mildmay of Apethorpe, 'a gay and gallant but unwilling bridegroom', full of ambition to make his way at court, preferably without the encumbrance of his quiet, unsophisticated wife. Life at court held no appeal for Grace, and it was

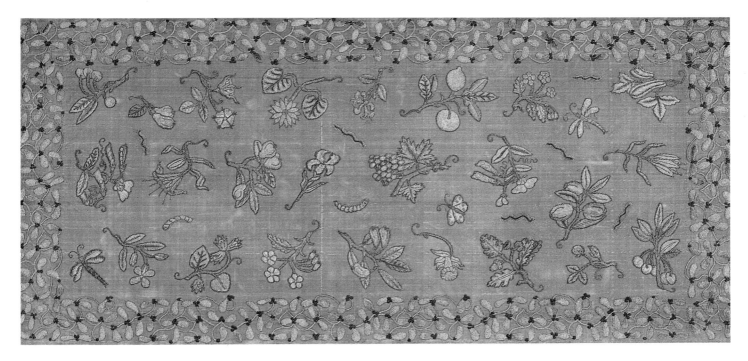

agreed that she should stay at Apethorpe with her parents-in-law. Here she played her lute, continued to sing psalms as well as songs, and study her herbals. 'Also every day I spent some time in works of myne own invention without sample [sampler] or pattern before me for carpett or cushion work, and to drawe flowers and fruitt to their life . . . all which varietie did greatly recreate my mynde, for I thought of nothing else but what I was doing'. Such happy, total absorption is one of the great pleasures of doing embroidery; the pattern takes shape as time slips by, and Grace appears to have found her solitary life rewarding rather than irksome.

While studying the herbals, she may have noticed pictures of plants suggestive of patterns, but with her aptitude for drawing she could devise her own 'carpett and cushion' designs without difficulty. The carpets would have been for the table rather than for the floor, and like the cushions they were probably worked entirely in canvas stitches or with 'slips' – motifs first worked in tent stitch and then cut out and applied to satin or velvet. There were ten tent stitch cushions in her father's inventory, and another dozen on a blue ground of which six were 'unmade upp', suggesting that the slips had yet to be applied.

Grace was unusual in making up her patterns without reference to her sampler, but Mistress Hamblyn would almost certainly have seen to it that her pupil made one. In the absence of any 'how to do it' books, a sampler was an invaluable record or *aide mémoire* of stitches, and also it served much the same purpose as an embroiderer's notebook today – gathering together all sorts of motifs, patterns and suggestions for future use.

We know from wills and inventories that samplers were made both by adults and by children during the sixteenth century, but only one dated example has survived. This is

Cushion at Hardwick Hall worked with flowers and fruit slips applied to tawny velvet within a mistletoe border

Mistletoe from Fuch's De Historia Stirpium, *1542*

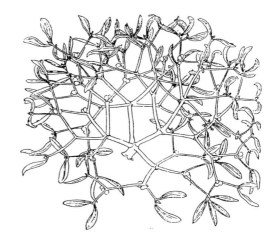

the famous sampler (now in the Victoria and Albert Museum) made by Jane Bostocke in 1598 for a girl named Alice Lee who was born in 1596. The complex stitches and patterns are crowded on to the rectangle of handspun and woven linen, with enough of each to show how it would have looked on a cuff or pillow cover. A strawberry pattern in detached buttonhole stitch leaves one fruit half finished and another waiting to be filled in, as if Jane were inviting Alice to prove her mastery of the stitch by completing them. Jane provides two further strawberry designs, altering the stitches and colourways, twisting the stems into different patterns and adding flowers and small flourishes. She improvises with carnations, grapes on a vine and pomegranates in a trellis, setting the patterns close together to vie with each other in complexity.

The random motifs in cross stitch at the top of the

Opposite *Jane Bostocke's sampler, dated 1598, was intended as a storehouse of patterns for future use. Here Belinda Downes takes the strawberry, knot, bird-in-a-tree, oak leaf and dog motifs as the basis for making new patterns for boxes or cushions*

sampler appear simple in comparison. The pet dog, Juno, the owl half-hidden in the oak sprig and the squirrel in the rose were intended perhaps to amuse Alice and provide easy models to get her started. Jane's most intricate patterns would have demanded considerable skill and concentration, hence William Barley's firm admonishment to the 'pretty maidens' copying designs in his book:

> Sitting at work cast not aside your looke
> They profit small that have a gazing minde
> Keep clean your samplers, sleep not as you sit
> For sluggishness does spoil the rarest wit.

Elizabethan parents and teachers were stern, demanding constant diligence and absolute obedience, and children's 'sluggishness' was not to be tolerated. 'It grieveth me to see you so sluggish', says another governess, the fictional Mistress Clemence, to her charges Fleurimonde and Charlote in *The French Garden*, a lively conversation manual written in 1605 by Peter Erondell, a Huguenot refugee. Mistress Clemence threatens to tell the girls' mother of their idleness, which puts them in a great flurry of activity: 'Sister where be our workes? I forgot my needlecase, take the silke . . . the crewel is not untwyned, it is all one . . . I have not my silver thimble, it is within my workbox'.

Summoned by their mother they show her their efforts apprehensively. Poor Fleurimonde's attempts at cutwork are immediately criticised: 'Methinks I espie a fault in it.' Fortunately the edge at least is reasonably well made, and

she turns to her other daughter, 'And you Charlote, where is your worke? Are your tapestrie cushens ended?' Charlote answers that she has only one left to do, and is quick with excuses, 'I lack silke, I knowe not what became of the cushen canvas, all of my gold and silver is done, I want more black yarne, I have not enough cruell.' 'Cruell', or crewel as we call it now, was handspun from long staple wool (worsted) similar in character to the yarn used in making the Bayeux Tapestry (which is, of course, not a tapestry, woven on a loom, but an embroidery, stitched with crewels on linen). There was just as much confusion between the two words in the sixteenth century as there is today, and Charlote's 'tapestrie cushens' were certainly not woven, but embroidered on canvas. The endearingly scatterbrained sisters appear to have passed the

sampler stage, and the materials suggest that they were working in several different methods.

After the hours spent learning and practising stitches it was rewarding to embark on decorative items, as a passage in *The Tale of Phylotus and Emilia* shows. Written in 1583 by Barnaby Riche, this diverting story is doubly interesting as it throws light both on needlework and on Elizabethan marriage customs. Set in ancient Rome, it tells of young Emilia whose father proposes her in marriage to his elderly friend Phylotus 'more for goods than goodwill . . . more for lucre than for love'. She pleads to be allowed to marry a younger husband of her own choice, but this is rejected, and so Emilia retires to her chamber to consider what possible advantages there might be in having an old but rich husband. First, she

thus with her needle to pass the afternoon with devysing of things for her own wearynge: and this likewise pleased her very well'.

If Emilia's samplers resembled Jane Bostocke's in the number of patterns they recorded she would have had a treasury of designs to choose from, and her wealth would allow her to buy the most luxurious materials to work them, together with laces and ribbons to trim up her creations. Once married to Phylotus, she could have purchased as many embroidered items as she wanted, but even so, like many of her contemporaries, she derived so much pleasure and satisfaction from her needlework that she preferred to 'devise' things to suit her own taste, embroidering coifs and other accessories herself.

The story turns into a hilarious romp of mistaken identities, and eventually Emilia succeeds in duping Phylotus and her father and marrying the suitor of her choice. Hardly any of Barnaby Riche's female readers were able to do this. Matchmaking was a parent's prerogative, and a good marriage in this status- and property-obsessed age meant one that would bring land, wealth and advantageous connections for both families. Like Emilia, most girls were betrothed as young as possible, with little or no say in the matter. Marriage was the only vocation for a gentlewoman, and the need for financial security, property and the related status, as well as a measure of freedom after being subjected to extreme parental strictness, weighed heavily in its favour.

Another diary, written by Margaret Hoby between 1599 and 1605, reveals the satisfaction many gentlewomen must have experienced when at last they became mistress of their own household. It also shows what an important part needlework played in their lives. Margaret was a rich heiress, and when, aged twenty-eight, she began her diary she had had ample experience of matchmaking parents and guardians. The first two husbands chosen for her had died young, and in 1596, at the age of twenty-five, she was reluctantly married to Sir Thomas Hoby returning with him to live on her estate at Hackness in north Yorkshire. Here she lived quietly but busily, supervising the household, overseeing everything that went on in the gardens, dairy, kitchen and stillroom, writing letters, and doing accounts. In a remote country district like Hackness, a great house provided the services of a surgery and dispensary for everyone living nearby and,

would be esteemed as the wife of a wealthy man with an impressive establishment, she would have servants 'so she would not have to beate her brains about the practising of housewiferie' and she would keep them hard at work without 'marring the beauty of her hands . . . Then she began to think what a pleasure it was to be furnished with sundrie sutes of apparell, that in the morning, when she should arise, she might call for what she should list accordyng to the tyme and fasshion did require'. Pleased at the thought, she imagines how each day, after dinner, she would 'seke out her samplers' to 'peruse' which pattern would 'do beste in a ruffe . . . whiche on a sleeve, whiche on a quaife [cap] . . . whiche on a handkerchief . . . and to sit her down and take it forth little by little, and

Above *Needle in hand, ten-year-old Jane Halswell shows off her embroidery of rose hips. British School, 1612*

Border from Egenolff's Modelbuch, *1537, depicting Phyllis teasing the elderly Aristotle*

Elizabeth Drury rests on a blackwork pillow showing off her richly embroidered *dress in Paul van Somer's portrait of 1610, the year of her death*

like Grace Mildmay, Lady Hoby was an experienced herbalist who could prescribe many simple remedies.

She also spent many hours on her needlework: 'I wrought [embroidered] till dinner time', 'I wrought with my maids', 'I wrought and instructed some of my family', she writes. Sometimes there were two needlework sessions on one day, and sometimes her chaplin, Mr Rogers, read aloud from Fox's *Book of Martyrs* or from his own sermons while she stitched. A devout Protestant, Margaret Hoby began and ended every day with prayers, she studied the Bible, and wrote her own sermons, but

Carnation and heart's-ease from Gerard's Herball

Details of James I sampler crowded with motifs and patterns including a *fashionable lady with a fan, a mermaid, shepherd, knots and flowers*

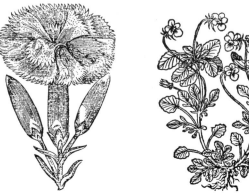

Above *Slip of a coach on a chair back at Hardwick Hall. Travel was slow, as Lady Hoby recorded in her journal*

Motifs from the Hardwick furnishings adapted by Belinda Downes

sometimes she turned to her herbal. By the end of the sixteenth century plant lovers and herbalists could study either Henry Lyte's *Niewe Herbal* of 1578, or John Gerard's wonderful *Great Herball* of 1597, if they had not found what they wanted in Turner's. The range of plants which could be adapted as embroidery patterns was increased by the images in these books, but sadly Margaret Hoby does not describe her designs or give details of what she wrought. The New Year gift list of 1600 records a 'snoskyn' (muff) of cloth of silvers, 'embroidered all over with flowers of Venice gold, silver and silk of sundry colours', offered to Queen Elizabeth by Lady Hoby, but there is nothing in the diary to say whether she embroidered such a muff herself, bought it ready-made, or commissioned it from a professional.

In London the widest range of embroidered items and

embroidery materials were found at the mercers and milliners in the 'Pawn' at the Royal Exchange, or in the smart establishments in Cheapside, where sellers of luxury goods displayed the latest fashions. Lady Hoby visited the Exchange near the end of 1600, and on 31 October noted the purchase of 'a New Year's gift'. The milliners specialised in choice items suitable as gifts, such as fans, brooches, 'curious imbroydered waistcoates' and gloves, sweetbags, coifs and sleeves (sold in pairs to be attached to the bodice with small ties known as points), all prettily decorated with needlework.

On another visit to the Exchange she bought a 'little spinning wheel' to take back to Hackness. Thread was spun by gentlewomen and their maids in many households, using the fibres both from flax or hemp, or from wool; and the ability to spin a fine thread was much admired. Until the mid-century this was done using a distaff and spindle, pulling the fibres out with one hand, twisting them deftly between finger and thumb, and winding them on to the spindle. It demanded patience and skill if the thread was not to break and unwind, but once the spinning wheel made its appearance the process became easier and quicker, as the new invention was designed with a foot treadle, leaving the spinster with both hands free to guide and twist the thread. Not only was the spinning wheel pleasant to use and attractive to look at, it meant that all thread could be spun more efficiently. Lady Hoby also supervised the maids at Hackness pulling hemp, which produced a coarser thread and fabric than flax, but was easier to grow and prepare for spinning.

While many households spun their own thread, weaving it into cloth was more likely to be left to a passing journeyman weaver, and late in the century there was even less incentive for home weaving when a whole range of linens, many of them imported from Flanders, became easily available. There were fine cambrics for blackwork, closely woven linens for cutwork, and even-weaves that were ideal for canvaswork, all of which could be bought at fairs, in the shops in the bigger towns, and from pedlars who travelled the countryside.

The pedlar Autolycus in Shakespeare's *A Winter's Tale* carried stock chosen to provide both basic essentials and 'trifles' to tempt customers living far from towns. He offered cambric, cyprus (a silk or linen fabric so fine as to be almost transparent), lawn 'as white as driven snow', silk threads, pins, and the steel poking sticks used to support ruffs, together with such covetable items as 'Perfume for a lady's chamber', ribbons 'all the colours of the rainbow', and embroidered smocks, stomachers and caps. Autolycus' silk threads would have been imported from the eastern Mediterranean. They came in skeins, either floss (smooth) or twisted in colours fancifully named such as watchet or popinjay blue, soppes-in-wine (carnation), lustie gallant (red) or murrey (mulberry). There were different qualities of black or sable silk, but in all of them the iron mordant used to fix the dye eventually rotted the thread, often leaving only lines of stitch marks to hint at the original effect. Gold and silver threads came from Venice, Lucca and Cyprus, their cost depending on the proportion of gold and silver in the wire used in their making. Once the wire had been drawn out to hair-like fineness by the wire drawers, it was wound on a core of yellow silk to produce threads that were not only beautiful, but pliable – an essential

A bright fire and a single lamp provide sufficient light for embroidery,

spinning and lace-making to continue after dark, as shown in Philip Galle's

engraving after Jan van der Straet. Note the carefully dressed frames,

the shears resting on the work-basket and the elaborate bed furnishings

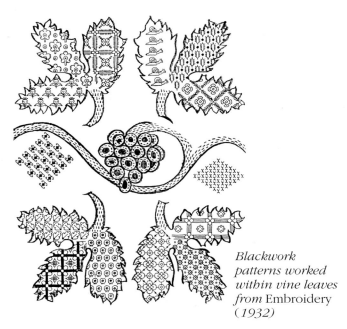

Blackwork patterns worked within vine leaves from Embroidery *(1932)*

quality in complex interlacing stitches.

Pins were indispensable, not only for sewing, but for fastening together the various bits and pieces that made up a fashionable outfit. Made of brass or copper alloy in varying lengths and thicknesses, they were sometimes fitted with beautifully crafted heads. In his *Description of England* (1587) William Harrison noted that pin-making had begun in England in the 1570s, and that the English pinners 'excell all nations'.

Autolycus probably carried needles as well, quite likely imported, since in this craft the English lagged behind the Germans and Spaniards, highly skilled in fashioning strong resilient needles from steel. These gradually replaced needles made from iron wire which were easily distorted and broken, and by Mary Tudor's time high-

quality needles were being made and sold in London in a shop owned by a Spanish Moor. The Spaniards had learned the difficult techniques of tempering steel from the Arabs, and in metalwork centres like Toledo and Cordoba they also produced scissors specially for embroidery and shears for cutting out fabrics. The intricate effects so much admired in blackwork, cutwork and embroidery in coloured silks and metal threads simply could not have been achieved without fine needles and razor-sharp scissors, and the new tools were prized possessions, kept in special cases to protect them from rust.

Some pedlars also offered a primitive kind of spectacles to help those with poor or failing sight. Originally invented in Italy at the end of the thirteenth century, the Elizabethan 'eye glasses' came mainly from the Netherlands; they comprised two magnifying glasses held over the bridge of the nose in cumbersome rims of horn, wood or leather.

Above *Detail of a blackwork pillow cover worked with flowers and birds, turkeys, cranes, doves and phoenix, possibly symbolising the Elements*

Right *Paddy Killer's Elizabethan tools include scissors, shears, thimble, fish-shaped needlecase and spectacles arranged on a cover with a blackwork edge. A cutwork trimming spills out of the work-box and ornamental pins are stuck in the pincushion*

The title page of Sibmacher's pattern book depicts a lady wearing nose spectacles, while another works on a frame with her pattern book resting on her work-basket

Below left *Tiny birds and lions decorate these etched and gilt scissors, knife and spike, part of a set kept in a leather case, c.1590. The etched and gilt shears are made in one piece and decorated with dancing figures*

The most intricate stitchery could only be worked in daylight, but this did not mean that embroidery stopped altogether at dusk. 'I wrought with my maids till almost night', wrote Lady Hoby, and presumably when it began to get dark they worked by candle- or lamp-light, backed up by a bright fire in winter. In summer, embroidery was taken into the garden, and indoors the chambers and parlours were lighter than ever before, because, as Harrison tells us, 'glass is come to be so plentiful' and

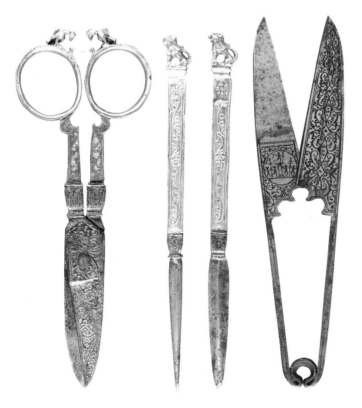

there were large windows to let in the light instead of small lattices filled with horn. Window seats and oriel windows were a feature in many new homes, though draughty in cold weather, they were ideal for close work.

Cold fingers must have been a problem for much of the year. In prison at Tutbury in the 1570s, Mary Queen of Scots describes her two little rooms as being 'so excessively cold especially at night, that, but for the entrenchments of curtains and tapestry . . . it would have been impossible for me to stay in them in the day time'. These 'entrenchments' would have made the rooms dark, and it is not surprising that she spent some time every day in Bess of Hardwick's chamber, where, as Bess' husband the Earl of Shrewsbury reported in a letter to William Cecil in March 1569, 'She useth to sit working with the needle, in which she delighteth, and in devising works'.

The year 1569 saw the beginning of Mary's fifteen years as a prisoner in the custody of the Shrewsburys, and there is no doubt that her interest and expertise in embroidery put her on good terms with Bess. Mary had been brought up at the French court, where textiles were lavishly used in interior decoration, and this was a subject of considerable interest to Bess, who aimed to make the houses she built the height of fashion in terms of design and decoration. Though twenty years older, there was much that Bess could learn from Mary, and it is not difficult to imagine the two ladies amicably 'devising works' together. This preliminary stage of a project, when the embroiderer first visualises an idea, and then works it out in practical terms, can be immensely exciting and pleasurable.

In the 1570s the process was all the more absorbing because of the wealth of motifs then to be found in book illustrations, especially in the enthralling new natural history and emblem books. Bibles, herbals and translations from classical literature had long been of great interest, as the woodcuts illustrating them were simple in outline, and easy to adapt as patterns.

Books were still rarities even in the grandest houses. In the detailed inventory made of Bess' possessions in 1601, only six books were mentioned, all kept in her chamber. Whether she owned a copy or not, Bess certainly adapted the flowers, vegetables and fruit in Mattioli's *Commentaries* of 1568 and 1572, and both she and Mary Queen of Scots made use of the lively woodcuts in the Swiss physician Conrad Gesner's *Icones Animalium* [Portraits of Animals] first printed in 1560, and the French naturalist Pierre Belon's *La Nature et Diversité des Poissons* of 1555.

Elizabethan readers, many of whom had never travelled further than the nearest town, found these books *wonderful* in the fullest sense of the word. Like the herbals and early maps and globes, they opened up new worlds alive with 'rare and strange curiosities' recorded on the voyages of discovery. While the renaissance naturalists aimed to describe and classify what they saw in an accurate and scientific manner, the legacy of medieval lore and legend was not easily forgotten, and 'monstrous sea serpents', mermaids, dragons and other marvels as improbable as those in the medieval bestiaries continued to appear alongside real newcomers such as reindeer from

Iceland, toucans from Brazil and beavers from Canada. These three appear in the panels of the Oxburgh hangings, the most celebrated of the 'works' devised by Mary and Bess, together with plants of all kinds and a whole zoo of other creatures, many chosen for their strangeness, but others, like the pet dog Jupiter, because they had a personal significance.

The key to many of the mysterious images that so appealed to Elizabethan taste was to be found in the emblem books which presented the reader with a series of 'speaking pictures' – images accompanied by mottoes and verses which quickly became so well-known that anyone seeing the picture of reading the motto immediately understood its significance. Emblem books had first appeared in Italy and France in the 1530s. The Queen of Scots would have been far more familiar with them than Bess, and she was also well versed in classical literature, and could have introduced Bess to stories from Ovid's *Metamorphoses,* which had been amusingly translated and were immensely popular at the time. Bess' adaptations of *Diana and Actaeon* and the *Rape of Europa* can still be seen on the long cushions preserved at Hardwick Hall.

The small panels of the Oxburgh hangings were worked mainly in cross stitch in coloured silks on canvas. Once the two ladies had decided on their subjects, they could call on professional help in getting them drawn out; and then they would have the pleasure of stitching the

An unknown lady (British School, c.1600) wearing a petticoat embellished with pearl-outlined obelisks or pyramids. The design lacks the assurance of the professionally embroidered jacket suggesting that the maker herself adapted *and drew out an obelisk* (below right) *found in F. Colonna's romance* The Strife of Love in a Dream, *(1592) or a pyramid or spire* (below left) *in Geoffrey Whitney's* A Choice of Emblemes *(1586)*

motifs in their chosen colours, and seeing the panels accumulate until enough were completed to arrange and mount as hangings.

Actual furniture was sparse even in the grandest homes, apart from beds, tables, stools and a few chairs, there were chests and perhaps a cupboard, and the impression of warmth, colour and comfort was created entirely by the textile furnishings. Tapestries, woven fabrics and the velvets, silks and the silver gilt threads used to embroider them were expensive; rich furnishings were highly valued, and looked after far more carefully than today. Nothing that could be re-used was ever thrown out: ecclesiastical vestments which had come into the hands of secular owners after the Dissolution of the Monasteries in 1538 were cut up and their brocade and cloth of silver displayed on cushions and hangings; in intriguing contrast, an extravagantly embroidered gown could be re-used as

an altar frontal – visitors to the little church of Saint Faith at Bacton near Hereford can still see the faded but enchanting flowers, birds and sea creatures on the petticoat thought to have been donated by Blanche Parry, one of Queen Elizabeth's ladies-in-waiting. In 1565 Mary Queen of Scots supervised the cutting up of a set of vestments to make flower-embroidered bed hangings as a present for her husband Lord Darnley, and during the 1570s, Bess re-used the sumptuous vestments from Lilieshall Abbey (acquired through her third husband, Sir William St Looe) in the remarkable hangings depicting the Vices and Virtues now at Hardwick. For such major projects, Bess would involve as many helpers as possible, not only her embroiderer, but her women and some 'grooms and boys as well'.

Only the very grandest establishments maintained a permanent embroiderer, but there were also competent

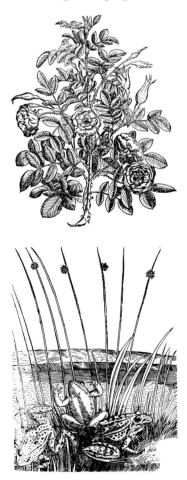

Left *Petticoat panel c.1600 embroidered with a figure representing astrology and emblematic motifs including cupids, thunderbolts, spiderwebs and armillary spheres*

Below *Rose and frogs from Mattioli's* Commentarii, *1568. The frogs appear in a panel of the Oxburgh hangings*

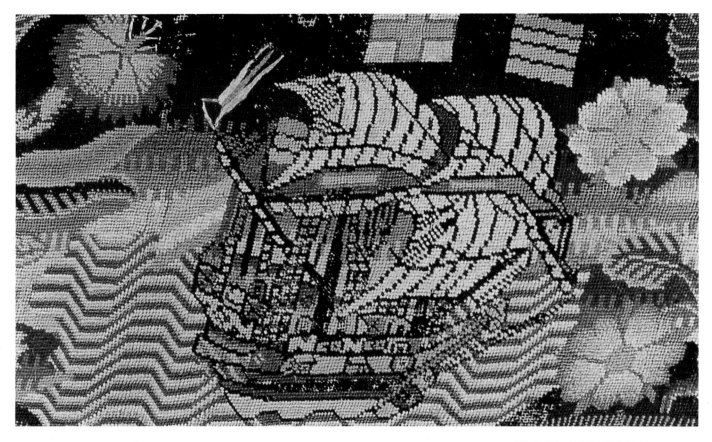

Above *A galleon in full sail on an early seventeenth-century valance*

Below *Monsters and mermaids seen in maps and globes were swiftly adapted for embroidery. Here Abraham Ortelius enlivens the Icelandic coast with strange creatures in Theatrum Orbis Terrarum, 1585. A similar monster appears on the cushion shown opposite*

Left *A mermaid border pattern and* (above) *a siren from the blackwork cover known as the* Shepherd Buss, c.1590

The Oxburgh hangings are rich in suggestions for pattern making. Here Belinda Downes uses bird and dog motifs from the hangings (including one from Jane Bostocke's sampler and another from the Bradford table carpet) to devise new designs

Below *Long cushion depicting* The Rape of Europa *based on a woodcut* (left) *in Jean de Tournes'* Metamorphose d'Ovide figurée (*1557*)

artisans who travelled from house to house, offering pattern drawing and making-up among their services. Failing this, the embroiderer could always transfer her designs from a herbal or printed pattern book by pricking and pouncing the outline herself, or by holding the page up against the light so the image could be traced.

The best pattern drawers were to be found at the Exchange in London. For a special commission – a set of

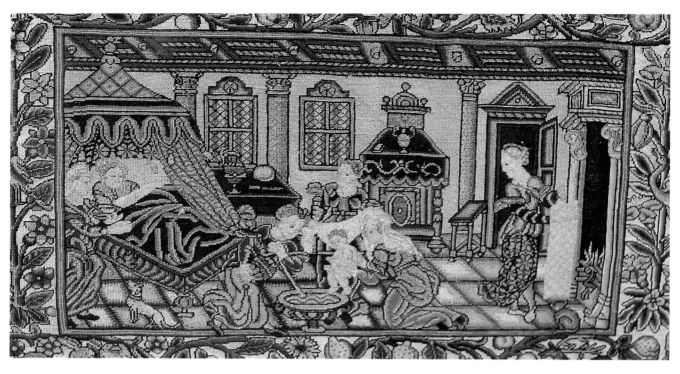

Above The Birth of Jacob *from a set of valances telling the story of Jacob and Esau, dated 1594. It is based on a woodcut* (left) *from Jean de Tournes,* Quadrins Historiques de la Bible *(1553), but the pattern drawer has elaborated the furnishings and introduced a dog and cat*

valances perhaps, or a gentleman's nightcap or a handkerchief ornamented emblematically – it was advisable to discuss the details in person, or, if that was not possible, to send specific instructions through a relative or friend. Those with money to spare could visit the professional workrooms to inspect the stock of tent stitch valances, table carpets, cushions and hangings, and if the examples on show failed to please, they could commission designs featuring a chosen subject, or their coat of arms.

A coat of arms made clear to everyone the importance of the bearer's position in society, and would be proudly displayed as often and as strikingly as possible. Impressively carved in wood or stone, engraved in silver, or painted in bright colours, they were particularly eye-catching in embroidery, the heraldic motifs and elaborate quarterings splendidly framed in strapwork patterns or standing out against a background of flowers. Professional workrooms could offer a wide selection of biblical, allegorical and mythological engravings for their clients to peruse. Once a subject was chosen, it could easily be adapted to the buyer's individual taste. Although the same groups of figures often appear, the dress of the characters and the backgrounds were always treated differently.

Tracing a design over a candle and against a window (above left), *pricking the pattern and pushing pounce powder through the holes* (below left) *from Allesandro Paganino's* Il Burato, *1527*

The central shield and supporting stag in this detail of a long cushion at Hardwick Hall refer to the arms of Bess of Hardwick's second husband, Sir William Cavendish, while the dog was the symbol of the sixth Earl of Shrewsbury, her fourth husband. The multiflowering trees and stylised hillocks remained popular motifs over the centuries (see pages 67 and 150)

Men of the Palmer family demonstrate shields emblazoned with their arms, motifs drawn from the Palmer Needlework (1625), a panel reflecting the passionate concern with heraldry

Many scenes were set in gardens or the countryside, and these provide a unique record of everyday pleasures and activities. The garden backgrounds show exactly how the pleasances so tantalisingly described by poets and foreign visitors were laid out; they depict in detail features such as elaborate knots – neatly clipped in evergreen herbs in patterns identical to the embroidery – fountains, covered walks and trelliswork arbours entwined with roses and honeysuckle. The country scenes are just as evocative, bringing alive all sorts of rural pursuits: farming, angling, falconry, and in particular hunting, one of the passions of the age.

These activities are set in idyllic, landscapes, with small fruiting trees and large flowers growing on rolling hillocks beneath a gold-rayed sun. Villages, churches, manors and windmills ornament the horizon, and streams leading into

Couples merrymaking in a garden, from a set of valances telling the 'Story of Lot', c.1600

31

pools and lakes add further colour and interest to scenes of high drama or peaceful rusticity. The long, narrow shape of the valances that hung pelmet-like from the roofs of four-poster beds was ideal for unfolding a narrative in a series of scenes, each one based on a separate engraving illustrating incidents in biblical stories, like those of Adam and Eve, or Solomon and the Queen of Sheba. Their popularity reflects the importance of Bible study at the time, while the huge interest in classical literature meant that mythological heroes and heroines were just as fashionable.

The domestic embroiderer was less likely to embark on large scale wall hangings, table carpets or sets of valances densely covered in tent stitch than to ornament her furnishings with slips which could be conveniently worked in a small frame. But the highly appealing effect of tapestries and embroideries displayed in other peoples' houses provided her with all sorts of ideas and motifs which could be incorporated into her own work. Thus an elaborate garden entertainment could be suggested by a simple arbour sheltering a pair of lovers, while a hunting scene complete with running hounds and mounted horsemen in pursuit of stags and wild boar could be evoked by a single stag outlined in pearls on a sweetbag.

The most popular motifs on dress and furnishings were flowers, but hops, pea pods, holly berries and fruit of all kinds came a close second. They reflect the interest in growing a variety of fruit and vegetables, and in every aspect of horticulture. 'It is a great fruite year all over', wrote Lady Hoby describing the Indian summer of 1603. In November that year 'Hartechokes' and raspberries and

Above *Cherries and hazelnuts from Jacques le Moyne de Morgues'* La Clef des Champs *(1586)*

Below *A hazel and honeysuckle design suitable for a child's dress based on a cover, c.1590*

white and red roses, including a cutting of a musk rose taken the previous winter, cropped and flowered a second time. The flowering season in British gardens then was far shorter than today, since there were hardly any of the plant introductions from the Americas and the Far East which we now take for granted: to embroider the shapes, shades and textures of flowers, fruit and vegetables was a delightful way of preserving summer's bounty.

Peas were popular motifs on dress and furnishings. Their decorative potential is brought out in this woodcut from Mattioli's Commentarii *(above right) and a* Booke of Divers Devices, *1598* (below). *In the unknown lady's portrait* (above left) *peas are combined with pomegranates in blackwork on the stomacher and sleeves. British School, c.1580*

Late sixteenth-century valances depicting rural pursuits (top left) *and huntsmen in classical dress chasing a dragon and lion through the same idyllic countryside* (bottom left)

– 2 –

The Stuart Embroiderer

She wrought so well in Needleworke that she
Nor yet her Worke shall ere forgotten be.
John Taylor, on Mary,
late Countess of Pembroke, 1630

The flowering of embroidery, which had begun in Queen Elizabeth's reign and owed so much to her enthusiasm for the art, continued unabated after her death in 1603, becoming if possible even more extraordinary. At the pleasure loving court of James I and Anne of Denmark embroidery remained the perfect medium for creating fashionable and ostentatious effects. Flights of butterflies shimmered across ladies' gowns, ripe cherries and currants glowed on jackets, and gentlemen could choose between clouds and rainbows, serpents and phoenix to sparkle on their nightcaps, or wear gloves round whose gauntlets a huntsman and his dogs ran in full cry. At home there were many gentlewomen who, like Lady Pembroke, 'their happy time most happily did spend' embroidering clothes and furnishings, and John Taylor did not exaggerate (in his much-quoted poem 'The Prayse of the Needle') when he remarked that without the needle his contemporaries would have

> No shirts or smocks from nakedness to hide,
> No garments gay to make us magnified.

The extent to which the gay garments really did 'magnify' their wearers and their self-esteem can be seen in countless early seventeenth-century portraits. 'Rich apparel', wrote Ben Jonson in *Every Man out of his Humour*, 'has

Coiling patterns in gold enlivened with bright leaves and berries were high fashion both for men and women in the first decades of the seventeenth century. Sir Peter Saltonstall (above) *chose green and gold for the flamboyant doublet worn in his portrait, British School, c.1610. The* embroidery on the man's nightcap (opposite top) *shows the splendidly eye-catching effect of vivid coloured silks, spangles and silvergilt thread on a* fine linen ground. Patterns for similarly stylised berries (opposite below) *appeared in Thomas Trevelyon's* Miscellany *of 1608*

An unknown lady wearing a bodice and coif worked with cherries. Note the cutwork on ruffs, cuffs and aprons. British School, 1624

Squirrels, flowers and birds worked on a glove

strange virtues; it makes him that hath it without means esteemed for an excellent wit . . . [and] sets the wits of the ladies at work that otherwise would be idle'.

Idleness was a sin to be avoided at all costs. 'My mother', wrote Anne Halkett (1623-99), 'kept a gentle-woman to teach us all kinds of needlework which shows that I was not brought up to an idle life'. With the rise of Puritanism needlework was seen as a safeguard against idleness, protecting against sinful sloth. It continued to be an essential part of any carefully brought up girl's educa-tion, as well as a way for a lady to show off her taste and status. For the young women growing up in the period of mounting uncertainty following James I's death in 1625, and in the turbulent years before and during the Civil War, it must have provided a valuable antidote to stresses and strain, and much needed distraction and relaxation.

Travel remained both difficult and hazardous, and though more coaches rumbled along the unmade roads, it was generally safer and quicker to go on horseback. For people living in the country, home was the centre; occa-sional meetings with neighbours broke the monotony, and visits to the nearest town were a rare and special

Intriguing motifs of clouds and rainbows could be found in Henry Peachum's emblem book, Minerva Britanna, *1612* (below). *The maker of the nightcap* (right) *added glittering worms and snails*

event. As the political situation worsened, it became more important for households to become self-supporting, and diligence and skill in gardening, herbalism, needlework and all the arts of 'huswiffrie' – cooking, conserving, distilling and laundering – were given resounding praise. In manors and farmsteads everyone was busy 'ere the Sunne doth peepe'. The ladies of the house tried out the delicious sounding recipes for distilling hyssop, thyme, lavender and rosemary 'after a new and excellent Manner' or making a 'Paste of Violets, Roses, Marigolds and Cowslips' from Sir Hugh Platt's *Delightes for Ladies to adorn their Persons, Tables, Closets and Distillatories,* and they varied the ingredients and exchanged receipts to make their own cures for freckles, scented pomanders and perfumed soap balls for washing their most delicate embroidered garments. These were made from expensive Castile soap melted down with aromatics such as rosemary while a far cruder soap, based on tallow and lye, was used for the main wash. Even with favourable weather this was slow and laborious. But at the end the satisfaction of seeing the clean linen set out to dry on the well-clipped dwarf hedges of the knot garden – as recommended by William Lawson in *The Country Housewife's Garden* of 1617 – was matched by the pleasure of laying embroidered sweetbags filled with herbs and spices in clothes chests and linen presses to scent the carefully folded smocks and sheets.

Beds were important status symbols. The grandest had the top sheets worked with a border in black- or white-work, matching pillowcases and an embroidered counterpane or quilt over the blankets, its colour and design complementing the valances and curtains. The impressively long lists of bed and table linen and garments of all kinds in inventories and household books speak of the embroiderer's pride in her home; the poetic descriptions of pillow beres, coifs and covers are redolent of the flowers and herbs in William Lawson's garden and John Milton's *Lycidas:*

> The white Pink and the Pansy freak'd with Jet,
> The glowing Violet,
> The musk-Rose, and the well-attired Woodbine,
> With Cowslips wan that hang the pensive Head,
> And every Flower that sad Embroidery wears. . .

Here 'sad' means dark as well as melancholy. Milton may well have been thinking of flower slips glowing on a satin ground of black, deep violet or crimson. In the Earl of Northampton's inventory in 1614 there was a 'longe Cushion of blacke Satin with Slippes, Flowers, Wormes and Flies of needlework unmade upp' and no less than thirteen sweetbags, the most elaborate of which was 'embrodered with highe embosted Mosseworke [raised embroidery] having two Sea Nymphes upon Dolphins and other Figures of Fowles'. There were waistcoats and nightcaps, napkins and covers in profusion, and yard

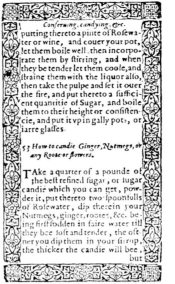 

Recipes from Delightes for Ladies, *1594, framed with a Tudor rose, fleur-de-lys and portcullis border reminiscent of an embroidery pattern*

Flower-de-luce and Tre-foy knots from The Country Housewife's Garden, *1617*

Mermaid and huntsman on early seventeenth-century sweetbags

Jollity at dinner in a picture in laid silks, c.1650

upon yard of velvet, some already embroidered 'with Flower de luces and Diamond worke'; a cloak with flower slips and borders in silver had been 'cutte forth into Pieces to embroider some Furniture in the House withal' – as in the previous century, needlework was re-used even in the grandest houses.

Of particular interest are the household books kept at Naworth Castle, a great border fortress near Hadrian's wall, about twelve miles north-east of Carlisle, the home of Lord William Howard, his wife Elizabeth, their eight children and numerous grandchildren and retainers. Everything that was needed, from vast quantities of food and wine, fruit trees, 'sheeres' for the garden, and 'a footeball' for the children right down to a 'key for the dog kennel door' was meticulously listed in the twelve surviving household books kept between 1618 and 1633. Lord William, for example, had literary, scientific and antiquarian interests, and built up a remarkable library. He was constantly buying books, among them 'an English Herball' acquired in 1629, probably John Parkinson's *Paradisus* which came out that year.

For us as embroiderers the numerous items for needlework are especially fascinating. They were listed under 'My Ladies' Expenses' and included quantities of needles, some with large eyes for 'crewells', pins, a bodkin, gold, silver and silk threads in variety, spangles and sequins, known as 'oes' at the time, 'an ounce of seed pearls', '2 yards of canvas and three ounces of silk', and 'sleeve silk for Sir Francis his Lady to work for my Lord'. This last was floss silk bought for Lady Elizabeth's daughter-in-law to work a present for Lord William.

'The Flower of the Sunne' and marigolds from John Parkinson's Paradisus

As well as embroidering herself, Lady Elizabeth paid for patterns to be drawn out on waistcoats and coifs, and for ruffs, smocks and pillowcases to be worked professionally. To balance these expenses, the family's clothes were frequently 'translated' or refurbished, and even Lord William's stockings were 'footed' to prolong their life! She settled the accounts for spinning and for weaving of linen for sheets, and purchased the blue thread for marking them. Naworth was situated 'in almost roadless country . . . islanded by dark woods' and like many country dwellers, she took the advantage of buying 'pins at the door' from a passing pedlar, and 'lawn at Lammas Fair'. For special items, such as fine lace thread, she would send to Carlisle or even to London.

Pedlars now reached the remotest parts of the country, supplying most of the embroiderer's needs apart from luxurious satins, silks and velvets. They specialised in inexpensive linens, and now carried useful items such as starch, indigo for dying and twopenny spectacles. Imported from the Netherlands in large quantities, these were still 'nose spectacles', but the best were now framed in wire which made them lighter and more comfortable. Superior versions could be bought from the London 'Spekticle Makers'; Lord William paid three shillings for one of the three pairs he acquired in 1629, and four years later he bought a pair of 'multiplying spectacles' presumably because he needed stronger lenses. By 1633 he had bought thirteen pairs, and perhaps some were borrowed for embroidery purposes. Certainly when, in 1631, Sir Henry Slingsby, the cavalier diarist, needed '6 pairs of specktacles to give away amongste my daughters', it must surely have been to encourage them in their needlework.

Each year in the Naworth accounts, there was a special section for money spent on lighting. To make the most basic candles, tallow was bought by the stone together with yarn for wicks. These melted alarmingly quickly, and

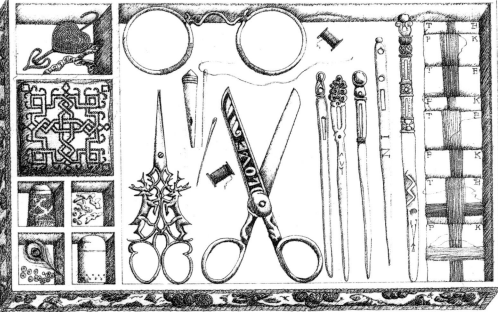

Above right *The fifteen-year-old Lady Anne Clifford painted by Van Belcamp in the* Great Picture *of 1646. Portraits of her tutor and governess, her Bible, favourite books and, on the table, her embroidery, evoke the years passed waiting for her inheritance*

A tape measure in the shape of an arrow, a pincushion with a knot outlined in pins, scissors, spectacles, bodkins, a mould for working detached buttonhole stitch, and threads wound on card depicted inside a raised work box

therefore needed constant attention if they were not to gutter and fill the room with evil-smelling smoke and smuts. Rush and oil lamps were also made, but these were just as messy and cast long shadows. For needlework the bright clear light of an expensive beeswax candle was far more suitable. In 1618 Lady Elizabeth paid the huge sum of nine shillings for 'a little looking glass', and she must have been delighted to find that it doubled the light of a solitary candle in her chamber. Though a great heiress herself, she was careful in her management of the household. Apart from her embroidery materials, her great extravagance was gambling at cards and backgammon, money for paying her debts being listed as frequently and meticulously as her favourite sugar candy.

The Naworth estates were close to the lands of another great northern family, the Cliffords, Earls of Cumberland. In the spring of 1616 the Howards entertained Lady Anne

Isaac Oliver's miniature of 1616 depicts Richard Sackville, third Earl of Dorset, in the sky-blue hose 'embroadered all over with sonnes Moones and starres of gold' mentioned in an inventory of his 'rich wearing Apparrel' in 1617. Many items were later re-used in furnishings for Knole

Clifford on a two-day visit. Lady Anne and her mother (the widowed Countess of Cumberland) wanted Lord William's support in winning back the Cumberland estates. These were Lady Anne's rightful inheritance, but her impetuous father (depicted by Hilliard as Queen Elizabeth's champion wearing a magnificent surcoat embroidered with emblematic devices) had misguidedly willed them to his brother.

Lady Anne tells of the visit in the diary she kept intermittently between 1616 and 1619. It shows how little had changed since Grace Mildmay's day half a century earlier. A girl's prime vocation was still to make an advantageous marriage, and despite her father's will, Lady Anne was a rich prize on the marriage market. She was won by Richard Sackville, the spendthrift third Earl of Dorset (the nephew of Lord William Howard). Spend he did, and when his own funds ran low, he determined to make her give up her claim to her estates and settle for monetary compensation. But Lady Anne knew that this money would immediately be squandered on high living at court and refused absolutely to give up her claim.

Her diary records the heartbreaking and seemingly endless wrangles over the estates, during which her embroidery provided valuable distraction. Eventually she retired to Knole in Kent, and there she immersed herself in making a set of cushions in Irish stitch, otherwise known as Florentine or flame stitch. The straight stitches used in this method are simple, but the stepped pattern can all too easily go awry if not counted accurately – and so demanding sufficient concentration to keep her mind off her problems. Thus on 22 March 1617, at the height of the argument, she began a new cushion on finer canvas than usual, perhaps because it needed closer attention. A few days later, after walking in the gardens at Knole with her acrimonious husband, she writes sadly, 'I wrought much within doors and strived to set as merry a face as I could upon a discontented heart'. Three months passed, and she was still 'working and being extremely melancholy and sad to see things go so ill with me'.

The embroidery sessions were enlivened when her attendants read to her from the Bible, from Montaigne's *Essays* or Spenser's *Faerie Queen*, and she records her happiness when, during a lull in the quarrel, her husband sat by her side reading while she stitched. Often when she walked in the park, she took her Bible with her as she was gradually reading her way through the Old Testament. She had a lively well-educated mind, and according to the poet and prelate John Donne, 'knew well how to converse of all things from predestination to slea (floss) silk'.

This was not as unusual as it sounds, since girls at that time were introduced to the Bible as soon as they could read. Children and adults, both Protestants and Catholics, spent hours each day studying the scriptures or in private prayer, and few Sundays passed without listening to sermons. Religion played a vital role in their lives, and

Above *The zigzag lines of flame stitch on the coverlet complement the bold decoration of this painted bed, c.1580-1639*

Above right The Whole Booke of Psalmes (*1646*) *in a binding with the owner's initials each side of a flowering and fruiting tree*

their Creator and the characters in the Bible were real to them, in a way that some might find difficult to understand today. Small wonder then that embroiderers should so often choose biblical subjects for pictures and caskets, or make bindings for Bibles and devotional books, together with cushions to support them and special bags to protect them when not in use.

Some of the most charming bindings cover the books exquisitely illuminated by Esther Inglis, the daughter of Huguenot parents who had fled from persecution in France and settled in Edinburgh during the 1570s. Like Peter Erondell, author of *The French Garden,* her father found employment as a schoolmaster, and her mother taught Esther the many different scripts she was to use in her books. In a portrait of her painted in 1595, she holds a book in a red binding ornamented with gold, which makes a bright contrast with the blackwork decoration of her stomacher. The carnation and honeysuckle in the background, their stems emblematically intertwined, suggest that the portrait celebrated her engagement to Bartholomew Kello, whom she married the following year. Similar flowers, with attendant birds and butterflies ornament the pages of the books that she was to make famous as the *Matchless Mistress of the Golden Pen.* Garlands of formalised roses, columbines, strawberries and pansies, strongly reminiscent of embroidery designs,

frame the elegant dedications written to flatter potential patrons, to charm them into buying the volume, possibly to commission another, or recommend the writer to their friends.

Her embroidery undoubtedly made these volumes uniquely personal, and this is probably why all but two were presented to royal patrons. Her first embroidered volume, bound in red velvet and ornamented with a Tudor rose and crown within a border of twining flowers and leaves was dedicated to Queen Elizabeth. It was a French version of the Psalms, written in 1599 in various scripts. Quite different in character, and the most enchantingly personal of all her creations, was the 'great little book' made in 1615 for her 'well loved Sonne Samuel

Detail of an early seventeenth-century pillow cover depicting the

creation of Adam, with a mermaid and animals patterned in coloured silks

Kello', copying the text of John Taylor's *Thumb Bible* of 1614. This really was the size of a thumb, a minute double volume (1¼ x 2in [3 x 5cm]) bound 'dos à dos' so that the Old Testament back cover formed the front of the New Testament, which the owner turned round to read. The worn green velvet binding, with only traces of a floral design remaining, speaks eloquently of constant use.

John Taylor's *Thumb Bible* contained dramatically shortened versions of the Old and New Testaments in doggerel verses which must have delighted young readers and stuck in their memories. For example, to condense the Book of Esther into four minute pages with two couplets on each page is no mean feat, but it was typical of John Taylor, a lover of jokes and pranks with a childlike sense of fun. While employed as a waterman on the Thames he once rowed from London to the Isle of Sheppey for a wager, using canes with dried fish tied to them as oars, in a brown paper boat which not very surprisingly disintegrated. He was a poet and pamphleteer with a genius for self advertisement, of interest to embroiderers because of

Opposite *Prayer books and Bibles were often decorated with printers' devices suggestive of patterns. These are from* A Booke of Common Prayer, *1629*

Above *Esther Inglis, Mrs Kello, wearing a copostain hat and embroidered stomacher, by an unknown artist, 1595*

Above right *Princess Elizabeth (daughter of James I and later Queen of Bohemia) by Robert Peake (the elder) c.1610, wearing a holly embroidered gown and holding a book the size of a 'Thumb Bible'*

Esther Inglis often ornamented the title pages of her books with exquisite flowers, birds and butterflies. This pattern for a notebook or album binding was inspired by her work. The simplicity of the design makes it easy to adjust the motifs to fit any size of book

Above *Abraham banishing his servant Hagar and their son Ishmael, depicted in fine tent stitch. The* *pattern is based on the figures in an engraving in de Jode's* Thesaurus (right). *Note the raised faces*

his long poem 'In Prayse of the Needle' which introduces the patterns in *The Needle's Excellency,* published in 1631 by James Boler, and as much a runaway success as the *Thumb Bible.* Boler's business was 'at the Sign of Marigold in (St) Paul's Churchyard' where many print-sellers offering engravings suitable for patterns were established, and where Taylor may well have acquired the information he needed. He promises the reader that the book will enable her to embroider any subject:

> Flowers, Plants and Fishes, Beasts, Birds, Flies and Bees
> Hills, Dales, Plaines, Pastures, Skies, Seas, Rivers, Trees,
> There's nothing near at hand or farthest sought
> But with the Needle may be shaped and wrought . . .

But, true to Taylor's form, this was yet another pleasantry, as the patterns in the book were almost entirely for lace and cutwork.

With his enthusiasm for words, he quite probably made up the names of some of the twenty-one stitches (Rosemary and Mowse stitch for example) which have puzzled embroidery historians ever since, but his comments on embroidery are none the less highly

perceptive. He expresses the child's point of view when he described how needlework skills were passed down from mother to daughter, or were taught by a 'mistresse' – either a governess or a school teacher:

And as a squirrel skips from tree to tree
So maids may (from their mistresse or their mother)
Learne to leave one worke and to learne another
For here they may make choice of which is which
And skip from worke to worke, from stitch to stitch,
Until in time, delightful practice shall
(With profit) make them perfect in them all.

The proof that they did eventually become 'perfect in them all' appears in the virtuoso stitchery on the many surviving samplers, and in pictures and cabinets in raised work. Taylor's image of the squirrel darting happily about brings alive the pleasure many children, and adults too, must have experienced, exploring the potential of stitches, and then using them imaginatively.

In contrast, the high standards demanded by governesses, and by teachers in the newly fashionable boarding schools, could equally well make embroidery a penance for those with little aptitude. In her memoirs, Anne Fanshawe, born in 1625, speaks appreciatively of her education 'which was with all the advantages the time afforded, both for working all sorts of fine works with my

Opposite below A tulip *dwarfs the lion in an engraving from* A Book of FLowers, Beasts, Birds and Fruit, *c.1665. Pattern drawers and amateurs used the motifs without changing the curious scale*

Above Belinda Downes *copied these animals and birds from an early seventeenth-century design inked on linen* (top). *Inspired by these motifs, she chose the elephant in devising her own pattern* (bottom)

Opposite *A spot sampler c.1640, worked with tiny patterns and random motifs including a man with a hawk, a cat, dog, stag, mermaid and flowers, in coloured silks and silvergilt on linen. Motifs from this and other spot samplers provide Belinda Downes with new ideas for pincushions, small boxes and cushions as shown here*

needle, singing, playing the lute and the virginals'. Even so she disarmingly describes herself as 'a hoyting girl', a tomboy who preferred 'running and all sorts of active pastimes'. The hours given up to needlework were even more tedious for studious girls like Lucy Hutchinson; 'For my needle I absolutely hated it', she wrote bitterly in her reminiscences, describing her resentment at being made to stitch, dance or practise the lute or harpsichord when all she wanted was to study. Born in 1620, she had learned to read and repeat sermons at the age of four, and admitted that 'the love of praise tickled me and made me attend more heedfully'. Had she been encouraged in the

same way by her needlework teacher, she might not have found her stitching so irksome. Many girls began sampler making at seven or eight, and if, as is likely, Lucy had to stitch one, she may have rebelled because she had to make a band sampler with meticulous examples of drawn and cutwork and row upon row of formalised fruit and flower patterns, rather than one with random motifs and patterns.

Known as spot samplers, these abound in the liveliest motifs – mermaids, birds carrying off huge worms and cherries, grasshoppers, insects and flowers inherited from the Elizabethans such as pinks and pansies, and novelties

Virtuoso use of detached buttonhole stitch and purl on a mirror frame. The *closed doors protect the glass, and the figures represent Europe and Africa*

such as striped tulips. There were obelisks, small buildings and people, especially couples probably representing the embroiderers' parents, all simply drawn in outline on rectangular pieces of fine unbleached linen. In contrast, the clusters of small scale diaper and other geometric patterns suitable for pincushions and sweetbags, generally worked in the lower half of the sampler, were a harder test. The patterns develop variations on earlier interlace and geometric designs with an inventiveness that is truly astonishing. Many of them incorporate stylised flower sprigs or heads, and for anyone interested in pattern making, I can think of few richer sources of inspiration.

Some samplers are so perfect that they were probably stitched by adults rather than children, and may well have been made by governesses or schooolmistresses to show to prospective employers as proof of their competence. Needlework featured prominently in the curriculum of the new boarding schools established round London early in the century. These schools quickly became fashionable with the daughters of the nobility and gentry, and for girls living in isolated parts of the country, they must have provided an exciting alternative to lessons with a governess.

At Mrs Perwich's select school in Hackney, established in 1643, her daughter Susanna first studied and then assisted in teaching. She was expert in 'fine embroidery, blackwork, whitework and work in colours', but sadly she had only a short while to impart her gifts as she died at the age of twenty-five. A poem written in 1661 celebrating her life and her embroidery describes how she could make,

> Pictures of men, birds, beasts and flowers
> When Leisure serv'd at idle hours,
> All this so rarely to the life
> As if it were a kind of strife
> Twixt Art and Nature: trees of fruit
> With leaves, boughs, branches, body, root
> She made to grow in Winter time
> Ripe to the eye . . .

How enjoyable it must have been for Susanna and her pupils to start on a picture or the panels for a cabinet or mirror frame! They could choose between tent stitch on evenweave linen so fine that remarkably realistic effects of shading could be achieved, or flat silk stitchery on satin, or the intricate technique known to its makers as raised work, but now more generally referred to as stumpwork, a misnomer, coined in the nineteenth century. Raised work was particularly inviting as there was no background to fill in, while the technique could display a wide repertoire of stitches. By about 1660 it had become a craze and embroiderers were competing in the creation of 'men, birds, beasts and flowers', each more ingeniously patterned, padded and manipulated than the last. For us, there is continuing delight in the extraordinary minuteness of the stitchery, augmented as we identify the characters in their beguiling world of fantasy.

Many designs were still based on the biblical and classical woodcuts used in the previous century. These, and more recently printed engravings, could be perused at the London print- and booksellers, who stocked a wide range of illustrated books and Bibles, together with separate sheets and sets of engravings. These sheets were intended for craftsmen of all sorts – tapestry makers, silversmiths and potters, as well as embroiderers. Some shops offered an additional service: marking out the pattern in ink on the linen or thick ivory satin. The haberdashers may on occasion have sold such ready-drawn designs together with a selection of silk and metal threads, seed pearls and pieces of mica (for windows) as an early form of embroidery kit.

By the time Hannah Smith came to make her cabinet (illustrated on page 7) she could choose from a splendid range of subjects. These included sheets of flowers, fruit, birds and animals, or books in which these motifs were

The lid of Hannah Smith's cabinet depicts 'Joseph being raised from the Pit' and sold to the Midianites. The draughtsman took the central group from Gerard de Jode's Thesaurus, but introduced two gentlemen in contemporary dress and a smiling sun

A spotted leopard sits peacefully by the grazing sheep in this tent stitch idyll. The initials and date suggest that it celebrates an engagement

charmingly grouped together irrespective of scale. Other sheets depicted Kings and Queens, the Five Senses, the Continents, the Elements, the Virtues and the Seasons – ideal for the sides of a cabinet, or the four corners of a mirror frame. On Hannah's cabinet, Autumn (Ceres) and Winter, warming his hands at a fire, appear on the sides, with Joseph being raised from the pit by his brothers on the lid, and two couples, Deborah and Barak, and Jael and Sisera, on the door panels.

Scenes from the Old Testament were by far the most popular. Incidents from the stories of Abraham, Isaac, Solomon and Sheba, or Ester and Ahasuerus recurred over and over again, always looking quite different because of the choice of stitches and colours. Hannah Smith depicts scenes which were far less frequently used. It is interesting to speculate whether she asked for them because they had special significance, or whether they were purchased from the print-seller's stock of ready-drawn designs. Much has been made of the Stuart embroiderers' preference for the heroic female characters in the Bible – models of virtue and fortitude, like Judith or Esther. The door panels of Hannah's cabinet celebrate the resourceful leadership of the Israelite prophetess Deborah, and the courage of Jael who lured the Canaanite captain Sisera to her tent and then killed him, but the choice of an all male scene on the lid – Joseph and his brothers – shows how dangerous it is to generalise.

The scene of Joseph comes from the most popular of all the engraved sources, Gerard de Jode's *Thesaurus* (Dictionary of Sacred Stories from the Old Testament),

first printed in 1585, available as separate sheets, or with the copious illustrations bound together in a handsome volume. If you consult this work it is clear at once that the engravings most often used for embroidery were also the most decorative. Bathsheba is shown bathing by an elegant fountain, and in Rebecca's meeting with Eliezer at the well, the camels provide an exotic note.

The professional draughtsmen knew shrewdly and exactly which scenes would attract most customers, and they could increase their appeal by altering the characters' classical dress to show off the latest fashions in periwigs, bucket boots and pearl necklaces. This resulted in a 'fancy dress' appearance, irresistible to young embroiderers, who portrayed strangely assorted outfits combining, for example, plumed helmets as worn by Roman soldiers with the latest petticoat breeches.

Pictures of couples exchanging gifts can be traced back to this

cutwork design from Sibmacher's pattern book of 1597

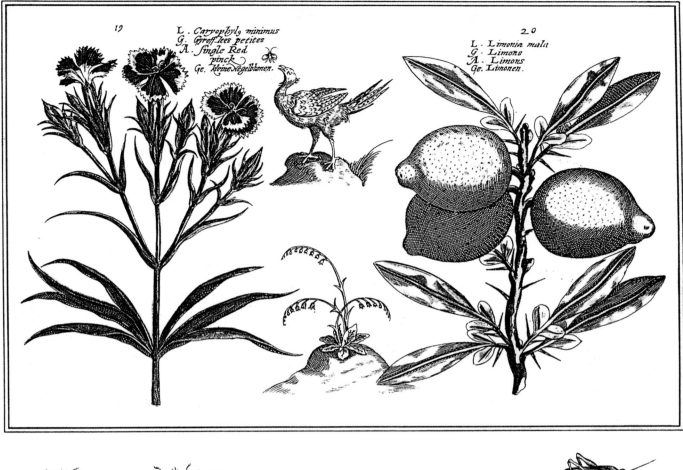

More authentic contemporary fashions appear in pictures depicting a gentleman offering flowers or fruit to a lady – made most probably as engagement presents. But whatever the main subject, the background was everywhere enlivened with an engaging cast of animals, birds and insects: lions, their curled manes contrived out of silk-covered purl (tightly coiled wire) or ravelled silk, were partnered with spotted leopards, antlered stags or unicorns; leaping dogs chased after hares while rabbits darted in and out of their burrows; birds too were arranged in pairs, kingfishers and finch-like parrots perching on sprigs set on small hillocks. Some of the grasshoppers and butterflies closely resemble the illustrations in Thomas Moufet's *Theatre of Insects* (1652) and others come from the pages of Crispin de Pass' *A Garden of Flowers* (1615).

Publishers, authors and print-sellers unashamedly pillaged earlier illustrations, altering them slightly in the process, and embroiderers could do the same, devising

Above top *Pinks, lemons and a jaunty bird from* A Garden of Flowers

Above centre *A grasshopper and dragonflies from the* Theatre of Insects *and* (above) *an 'insect' box design inspired by them*

patterns without recourse to the professionals, simply by using books in the family's possession. That they did so can be seen in some endearingly naive examples, as in a picture where a rainbow motif, traced or remembered from the illustration in an emblem book, or seen in a friend's embroidery, has been misunderstood and reversed to resemble a hammock strung up amongst the stars. In one highly idiosyncratic picture, faces, possibly portraits, peer out of the centres of large scale sunflowers growing in the background of a scene in which Moses is found by a fantastic rockery pool glittering with mica.

More formal portraits, often framed in an oval cartouche, were also popular. Sadly the identity of most of the sitters has been lost, though some are said to represent Elizabeth Coombe, a well known embroiderer of the day. It is curious how many of the male biblical characters in these scenes bear some resemblance to Charles I or Charles II. Portraits of both monarchs were occasionally stitched, and are instantly recognisable, but embroiderers sometimes expressed their loyalty to the Royalist cause through emblems or hidden images, as in a box made in 1660, the lid of which opens to reveal a tray lined with a crude drawing of the empty throne outside the Banqueting House, after the execution of Charles I. Remaining in the possession of its maker's family, the box (shown opposite) is still in pristine condition as it was kept under a pink taffeta cover in a specially made oak container. The embroidered panels depict scenes from the story of Isaac, and the colours remain as fresh as they were in the 1660s.

Above The Finding of Moses *(c.1650). Raised work with metal threads, coral and mica*

Below *The smiling sun and border motifs in this illustration from Elias Ashmole's* Theatrum Chemicum *(1625) resemble contemporary embroidery designs*

Above *Raised work-box, 1660, depicting scenes from the story of Isaac. The doors open to reveal drawers, some containing secret hiding places*

Left *Cupid aims at the Wise and Foolish Virgins drawn inside the box* (above) *and is reflected on the mirrored sides of the tray. The empty throne refers to the execution of Charles I*

It is easy to imagine the delight of its maker, or of Hannah Smith and other girls of their age, when the panels they had worked so hard to complete came back from the joiner or box-maker, beautifully mounted on the cabinet, and edged with shimmering silver braid. What excitement there must have been when they opened the doors to reveal rows of little drawers, ornamented with laid silk, one of which might conceal a hiding place for small items of jewellery. The cabinets were used to keep their owners' most precious possessions, toys and pretty conceits – an embroidered frog or bunch of grapes, or a bird whose folded lace stitch wings concealed a silver thimble. Martha Edlin's well documented cabinet (preserved with her samplers and beadwork jewel box in the Victoria and Albert Museum), completed in 1671 when she was eleven, contains a delectable collection of playthings and useful but decorative items – a needlecase and pin cushions, together with a set of miniature silver including a pair of candlesticks and a tea and chocolate pot, all marked with her initials, given to her as a reward when her project was complete.

In stumpwork, the soft seductive sheen of the pale satin

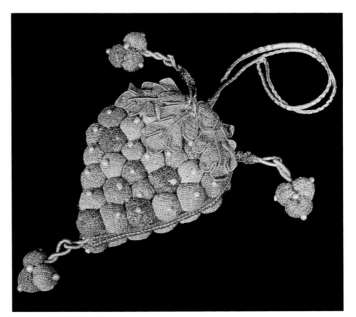

Detached and padded buttonhole stitch in coloured silks and silvergilt form the grapes in this

exquisitely made early seventeenth-century concertina purse with a plaited drawstring handle

Right *Crewelwork feathers ornament the hangings of this striking four-poster bed at Doddington Hall, Lincoln*

A 'bed royall' with plumed roof from Randall Holme's Academy of Armoury, *1688*

ground and the subtle colour gradations of the floss and twisted silks intensified the glitter of silvergilt threads, beads and spangles, especially in the fantastic fountains and rockery pools – the haunt of mermaids, seahorses and gaily patterned fish – favourite features at the base of mirror frames. Mirrors were then the height of fashion, but the quicksilvered glass was still extremely expensive. Often they were set in a wide embroidered frame opulently finished with tortoiseshell, silver or japanning

Mermaid motif from a mirror frame

which heightened their light reflecting quality. Beads had a similar effect, and these could be strung on linen thread or wire, either couched down to cover the motifs, or twisted and looped into three-dimensional flora and fauna.

In *The Gentlewoman's Companion* written in 1675 by the schoolmistress Mrs Hannah Woolley, this technique was described as 'All kinds of Beugle Work upon wires or otherwise'. A kindly and perceptive teacher, Mrs Woolley offered a well-rounded if not intellectually very ambitious education; the wide choice of embroidery methods and other crafts in her curriculum would have been popular with parents, and undoubtedly contributed to the success of her school. She offered her charges the opportunity to learn 'All Works wrought with the Needle, all Transparent Works, Shell-Work, Moss-work, also cutting of Prints and adorning Rooms or Cabinets or Stands with them . . . All manner of pretty Toyes for Closets. Rocks made with Shells . . . Frames for Looking-glasses, Pictures and the like. Feathers of Crewel for the corners of Beds'.

Plumes of real ostrich feathers, set in decorative holders,

were an impressive and fashionable feature, crowning beds hung with braid-trimmed hangings of velvet or damask. However, these were the speciality of professional embroiderers and upholsterers, and Mrs Woolley must have been referring to embroidery in crewel wools in a curling feather design. In *The New Atlantis* (1627) Sir Francis Bacon described 'Stuffs . . . with dainty Works of Feathers of wonderful Lustre', and this gloss or lustre was one of the most attractive characteristics of the crewels which the Stuart embroiderers used to make engagingly warm and colourful bed hangings. They were firmly twisted, which meant that the stitches and patterns were defined with a crisp precision that is difficult for us now to reproduce, using the softer yarns sold under the name of crewels today.

Although many of the motifs favoured in crewelwork were identical with those of canvas- and stumpwork, their effect was dramatically different, since they were generally worked on a larger scale and on new material imported from Bruges. This was a hard-wearing, natural-coloured twill with a cotton weft and linen warp and a distinctive diagonal weave; it was agreeable to work on and provided the perfect background to show off the texture and deep rich colours of the crewels. Both fabric and yarns were inexpensive, and the effect was delightfully novel and fresh looking.

Households that spun their own wool generally sent it away to be dyed, though it could be done at home, using madder roots for red, fermented woad leaves or indigo imported from India for blues, and saffron or weld for yellow. Green, made by covering blue with yellow, was by far the trickiest colour, and even when professionally dyed, it tended to fade back to blue, so that the original effect has long been lost. When new, the colours had a glowing intensity on the pale ground, and soon the tent stitch furnishings of the Elizabethans began to look old fashioned and over worked.

Yet the love of inventive stitchery remained as strong as ever, and some embroiderers, freed from the tight grid of canvas, found fresh possibilities in the twining stem designs so delicately and minutely worked by their grandmothers. They looked anew at the swirling leaves in the great vendure tapestries from Flanders which could transform a room into an enchanted woodland glade, and at the stylised trees crudely painted on tough linen hangings that were a substitute for tapestry in less well-to-do

Each leaf is differently patterned in crewelwork in this mid-seventeenth-century curtain at Breamore House, Fordingbridge. Squirrels were favourite motifs (see illustrations on pages 44 and 48) reflecting the vogue for keeping them as pets. One can be seen on page 86

Oak leaves on a printed box lining paper, 1615

Above *'Orientalised' oak leaves on a crewelwork curtain*

Below *Crewelwork stitch diagrams for stems from* Embroidery, *1932*

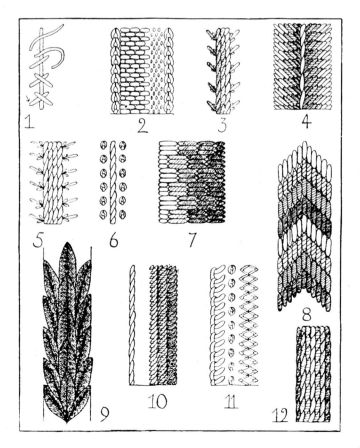

homes. Little by little they transformed this 'forestwork' – the evocative term for designs rich in foliage – first by stitching exuberantly patterned oak leaves and flowering stems in deep blue, green or red crewels, and then, later in the century, by adding outlandish birds, flowers and trees growing from fantastic rocks, so creating ever more entrancing effects.

These motifs can be traced back to the designs ornamenting porcelain and lacquer imported by the Portuguese from China and sold in the 'China Shops' at the Royal Exchange. When Sir Thomas Roe went to India as James I's ambassador to the Mughal court in 1615, he expected to find a treasure house of these Chinese wares, for like most Europeans he had only the haziest notion of far eastern geography, and imagined that the arts and crafts of China, Japan and India would be identical.

Looking there for rarities to send home to his wife and friends, he would have inspected the Hindu hangings with their enigmatic scenes crowded with figures painted in white on dark red grounds. Intriguing, certainly, yet they bore no resemblance to the exotic oriental art he had expected to find. The directors of the East India Company experienced far greater disappointment, as they had hoped to make a handsome profit trading in these hangings. However, knowing of their customers' fascination with the legendary world of Far Cathay they decided to provide them with appealingly oriental-looking designs. They began by reversing the colourways, so that instead of figures, there were flowers and branches painted in brilliant colours on white grounds. Almost at

once the mild public interest changed to a passionate desire to acquire sets of these charming 'chintzes'. In the 1660s, to capitalise on the success of their idea, the directors started sending out actual patterns 'in the China fashion' for the Indians to copy.

Seeking suitable models they turned to the leafy designs which Stuart needlewomen had been elaborating in crewels for the past three decades. On to these they grafted spectacularly exotic flowers, amongst which flew crested birds with gorgeous plumage and sweeping tails. Puzzled by these fictitious creations, the Indian craftsmen misinterpreted some motifs, and altered others, adding their own imaginative touches to create hangings that were neither western nor eastern, but an irresistible mixture of the two.

Quite unaware of their predecessors' contribution to the design of these seductive 'chintzes', later Stuart

Above *Belinda Downes' drawings based on the Elizabethan Bradford table carpet* (top), *and on the Ashburnham and Abigail Pett hangings* (below) *illustrate the growing fascination with oriental motifs, such as clouds, rocks and multiflowering trees*

Left *Late sixteenth-century Chinese wine jug decorated with stylised clouds. These became a popular motif in embroidery*

57

embroiderers found in them a thrilling new source of inspiration, and, sensing a craze, the professional draughtsmen quickly set about providing fashionable 'Indian patterns' for them to work. Pattern drawing was an increasingly competitive business. To attract new customers and retain old ones, print-sellers and haberdashers began advertising additional services on offer to the discerning embroiderer. Among the haberdashers was George Paravicini, whose London shop must have been an enjoyable place to browse in. His trade card describes him as a supplier of 'All sorts of India Patterns' and a 'Cutter and Raiser of Satin' meaning that he stocked not only markedout designs, but worked examples to show how they looked when complete – a sure way of promoting sales.

His card was at one time in Samuel Pepys' possession – it is still preserved in the Pepys Library at Magdalene College, Cambridge – and it may well have been from

Paravicini that his wife Elizabeth acquired the patterns for cushions which caused one of the couple's many disagreements during the year 1663. Pepys records 'She and I did jangle mightily about her cushions which she wrought with worsteds the last year', adding irritably 'which are too little for any use'. Embroiderers are quick to take umbrage when work, on which time and trouble has been lavished, is criticised and it is easy to imagine how upset Mrs Pepys must have been. There is no mention of further needlework in the diary until January 1665, when Pepys describes how 'she works like a horse at her hangings for our chamber and bed'.

Early eighteenth-century crewelwork hanging, one of a set depicting exotic flora and fauna and chinoiserie buildings. Note the continuing convention of the shaded hillocks

It is tempting to imagine that these were in crewelwork, inspired perhaps by the Indian painted calico which he and his wife chose together on 5 September 1663 to line her study; but if this were so they would surely have been mentioned before. Apart from this, a set comprising top and base valances, a coverlet and curtains was a major undertaking, and for Mrs Pepys to have completed such a time-consuming endeavour might seem out of character for one not noted for her perseverance. In matters of interior decoration Pepys was difficult to please; he had a keen eye for the latest trends, and was eager to try them out at home, so it is good to hear that he was in the end 'mightily pleased with what my poor wife hath been doing with her own hands like a drudge in fitting the new hangings of our bedchamber' – whether she herself had embroidered them or not.

During the 1660s there was further excitement for needlewomen and followers of oriental fashions when gorgeous silk embroideries from China began to appear in London. John Evelyn was one of the first to see these stunning novelties, when on 22 June 1664 he was shown a consignment of 'rarities' sent from the Jesuits of China and Japan to Paris, and brought from there to London. The most amazing were 'Glorious vests wrought and embroidered in cloth of Gold, but with such lively colours, as for splendour and vividness we have nothing in Europe approaches'. The Chinese had been masters in the art of silk embroidery for centuries, and Evelyn admired their skill in 'Flowers, Trees, Beasts, Birds etc: wrought with sleve silk (floss) very naturall'. The exquisite stitchery and liveliness of the Chinese designs provided inspiration for many dress accessories and furnishings, among them the fire-screen on page 69.

When in 1688 William and Mary came to the throne, interest in chinoiserie furnishings was further boosted by

Lions still linger on the shaded hillocks in this Queen Anne pastoral scene in flat silk stitchery

their enthusiasm for all things oriental. Queen Mary was a skilled needlewoman, and at Hampton Court she would sit with her Maids of Honour while one of them read aloud 'some book that was lively as well as instructing'. Celia Fiennes, on a visit to Hampton Court in 1712, saw one bedchamber in the Queen's lodging hung with 'Indian embroydery', and in the dressing room of the Queen's closet 'the hangings, chaires, stools and screen the same all of satten stitch done in worsteads, beasts, birds, images and Fruites all wrought very finely by the Queen and her Maids of Honour'.

Earlier on that same journey Celia Fiennes stopped at Mr Ruth's house at Epsom, and her description of the interior shows how much the embroidered furnishings contributed to the elegance and comfort of the 'new and neate' houses built in the reign of Queen Anne. She admired wall and bed hangings in cross stitch, 'cusheons' in the window seats, stools with 'crostitch true lover knotts' and 'many fine pictures under glasses of tentstitch sattinstitch gum and straw-work', and 'India' flowers and birds.

Tent stitch and cross stitch furnishings had come back into favour at the end of the seventeenth century. They looked particularly handsome on wing chairs, and suites of furniture comprising a sofa and a dozen or more chairs, which were now for the first time comfortably upholstered. Celia Fiennes does not record the subjects of the tent and satin stitch pictures she saw, but if they had been recently worked, they were far less likely to depict Old Testament scenes than mythological, pastoral or arcadian themes – which were to be the favourite subjects of the Georgian embroiderer.

The Georgian Embroiderer

See what Delights in sylvan scenes appear
Descending Gods have found Elysium here.
'Spring Pastoral', Alexander Pope, 1713

In March 1712, two entertaining letters appeared in Addison's periodical, *The Spectator*. The first, on 11 March, gave 'a picture of a life filled with a fashionable kind of gaiety and idleness'. It was the diary of Clarinda, a rich, empty-headed young lady who had perfected the art of wasting time. While in town she amused herself visiting friends, playing cards, discussing fashions – an hour is spent moving a beauty spot round her face before eventually fixing it above her right eyebrow – going to the theatre, reading romances and dreaming of her heart-throb Mr Froth. Friday's entry reads, 'One in the after-noon. Called for my flowered handkerchief. Worked half a violet in it. Eyes ached and head out of order. Threw by my work, and read the remaining part of *Aurangzebe*' (this romantic tragedy by Dryden was the hit of the season). After two more days of frivolity she concludes, 'I scarce find a single action in these five days that I can thoroughly approve of, except the working of the violet leaf, which I resolved to finish the first day I am at leisure'.

What a contrast with the pious Lady Hoby's journal a century before! Times had changed, and for the growing class of people described by Defoe as 'the middling sort who live well' – and Clarinda was certainly one of these – life was now leisured and secure. To emphasise this change, Addison ended the 11 March issue with a verse in praise of the industrious Countess of Pembroke, whose needlework had been celebrated by John Taylor a century

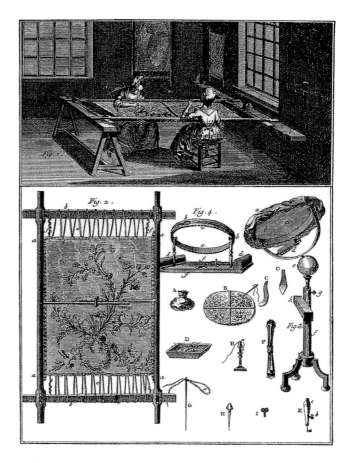

Professional embroiderers at work, with frames and tools for beading and tambourwork from Receuil des Planches, *1762-67*

The idyllic pastoral theme was celebrated by embroiderers and poets throughout the eighteenth century. Mary Davison's picture recalls lines in Ambrose Philips sixth Pastoral: *'Soft on a cowslip bank my love and I / Together lay; a brook ran murmuring by: / A thousand tender things she said / And I a thousand tender things replied'. The piping shepherd and his shepherdess may represent Daphnis and Chloe, or Orpheus and Eurydice*

before (see page 34), and who would have been appalled by Clarinda's frivolous wasting of time.

Life filled with 'a fashionable kind of gaiety' seemed more attractive to Clarinda's generation than the routine of housekeeping in which their grandmothers had been so actively engaged. Living in the country, Clarinda thought longingly of London and its excitements. The range of goods in the shops was wider than ever before, and consequently there was no longer the same necessity to make everything at home. Addison's next target in *The Spectator* (17 March 1712) was a lady who persisted in doing so, to cloak her extravagance 'under pretence of frugality'. 'Tis incredible what sums she expends on embroidery', laments her husband, describing how 'she keeps four French protestants [these would have been highly skilled Huguenot embroiderers] continually employed' making superfluous furnishings. This is passed off as a 'notable piece of good housewifery because they are made at home, and she has had some share in the performance'. An 'immoderate fondness' for embroidery!

The Clarindas of the day would doubtless have found this lady's out-moded attitude amusing, without realising that both she and they were being ridiculed. They would have revelled in yet another *Spectator* letter (13 October 1714) from a lady of the older generation, complaining about the behaviour of her two nieces who fritter away their time in gossip, visits and dress, yet 'go to bed as tired with doing nothing, as I am after quilting a whole underpetticoat'. She appeals to the editor to reawaken their interest in 'the long neglected art of needlework'.

In teasing tones Addison answers that embroidery is indeed an excellent way of keeping 'pretty creatures' out of harm's way, and tongue-in-cheek proposes 'laws' to restore the art. Mothers, he suggests, should insist that their daughters embroider their gowns and stomachers before being allowed to receive admirers, and work layettes before they may marry. His reply is of particular interest since he describes the subjects that appealed most to the needlewomen of his day. These included fruit, flowers and country themes with amorous overtones. 'Your pastoral poetesses may vent their fancy in rural landscapes', he wrote, 'and place despairing shepherds under silken willows or drown them in a sea of mohair'.

Addison's 'pastoral poetesses' were following an established tradition. The Elizabethans had depicted rural landscapes complete with shepherds and milkmaids on valances and table carpets; Stuart embroiderers continued with pictures and cabinets. These subjects were depicted throughout the eighteenth century, reflecting the general interest in pastoral themes in tapestries, porcelain, painting, music and literature, and even in the making of gardens which resembled country farms and arcadian landscapes.

Pastoral poetry was especially popular. In Addison's day

Left Inspired by the ninth of Virgil's Eclogues, *the frontispiece to Stephen Switzer's* The Practical Husbandman and Planter *(1733) celebrates perpetual spring - a favourite subject with Georgian embroiderers, who found many ideas for patterns in book illustration*

many embroiderers read of love-sick shepherds in the young Alexander Pope's *Pastorals* and delighted in recreating his 'sylvan scenes' in needlework, whose gentle charm matches the deceptive simplicity of the verse. Couples masquerading as shepherds remind us of earlier lovers in Stuart pictures as they stroll, or sit together on turf 'with rural dainties spread'. They appear on countless screens, on card tables and on the backs of chairs and settees, making it clear that the art of needlework, far from being 'neglected' or 'decayed', was flourishing. There were still plenty of 'exceedingly nimble fingered' embroiderers of both generations who spent happy hours working furnishings and dress accessories such as stomachers, aprons and handkerchiefs, not merely as a sign that they were ladies of leisure, but because it gave them pleasure.

Canvaswork was in favour with the most sought after designers and architects, a vogue encouraging domestic needlewomen who could follow high fashion at a fraction of the cost incurred when professionals were employed. Large-scale projects such as carpets and hangings were undertaken at home, as were sets of upholstered chairs, often with settees and stools en suite, whose elegant shapes showed off the textures, patterns and brilliant colours to perfection. Cabinetmakers understood how well canvaswork complemented their creations, and upholsterers were adept at mounting and finishing it to the best advantage.

Some ladies selected their patterns first, worked them, and finally had furniture made to suit their embroidery.

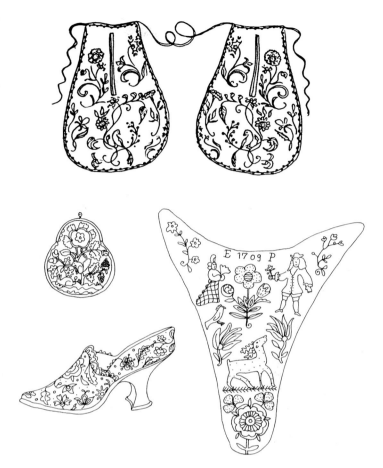

Early eighteenth-century stomacher, shoe, purse and pockets worn tied round the waist under a gown – useful for holding small items

Opposite *The frontispiece to Jonas Hanway's* Journal *(1753) depicts a fashionable town lady visiting the country accompanied by her pet dog and monkey*

Apron embroidered in coloured silks by Miss Rossiere for Miss Rachel Pain on her marriage with Miss Rossiere's brother, c.1736

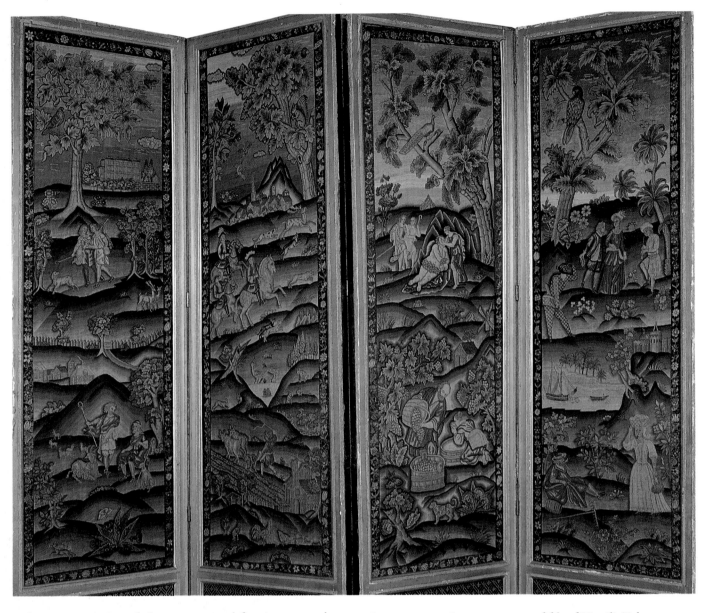

Others commissioned the pattern and furniture together. Today this would be exorbitantly expensive – we are more likely to make covers and panels for existing pieces, or make do with ready-made items, easily available, but doing little to enhance the finished work. We might well envy the Georgian embroiderers the excitement and pleasure of choosing designs and colour schemes in consultation with experienced craftsmen, who would consider the pattern in relation to the furniture it was to adorn.

A superb example can be seen in the beautiful six-fold screen worked by Julia Calverley in 1727 (seen above). The tall panels depict scenes of country life, set one above the other, and loosely connected by a common skyline and rolling hillocks animated with large decorative trees and small buildings. The effect is reminiscent of an oriental lacquer screen, emphasised by the choice of japanning for the framework, with each panel enhanced by a narrow black border painted with bright flower sprigs, whose colours pick up those of the embroidery

Country pursuits ornament the first two panels of Julia Calverley's tent stitch screen, signed and dated 1727. The third depicts grape harvesting and the drunken Silenus from the fifth of Virgil's Eclogues, while the fourth introduces a note of fantasy with palm trees on a distant shore, a piper and a harlequin, drawn from a theatrical print

and provide an exquisite finishing touch.

Since 1755 the screen has been at Wallington in Northumberland, brought there by Julia Calverley's son, Sir Walter Calverley Blackett, together with a set of ten large wall panels also made by her. These depict exuberant branches rising from the traditional shaded hillocks, and bearing native and exotic blooms recalling the patterns of the Indian painted chintzes and crewelwork hangings, but worked entirely in cross stitch in wools and highlighted with silk on a white ground. They were originally designed for the drawing room of Lady Calverley's new home at Esholt Hall near Bradford, and were three-and-a-half years in the making – their completion on 27

February 1716 being proudly recorded in her husband Sir Walter's *Memorandum Book.* Their sophisticated design suggests that, like the screen, they were drawn out by one of the foremost London firms.

The rural scenes on the screen are of special interest, as they were closely related to the enthusiasms of Lady Calverley and her husband. Five were adapted from the illustrations in Virgil's *Georgics* and *Eclogues,* translated from the Latin and published by John Ogilby in 1654. The *Georgics* described agricultural pursuits such as bee keeping and the making of baskets and farm implements, and the *Eclogues* recounted the discussions of two shepherds on various topics including the miseries of civil war. The Civil War had taken its toll on the Calverley family, and their Yorkshire estates had declined severely as a result of heavy fines during the Commonwealth, but they were restored by Sir Walter Calverley's careful management. They would both have appreciated the parallel

Left *The goat-herds on the left panel of the screen* (opposite) *were drawn from this illustration by Francis Cleyn in Ogilby's translation of Virgil's* Eclogues

Below *Harlequin and other Commedia del Arte figures were popular in all the decorative arts. Here they are embroidered in whitework on an early eighteenth-century apron*

Embroiderers found inspiration for pictures and furnishings on a pastoral theme in books, poems and engravings like these idyllic scenes by Watteau. Their needlework captures the bliss expressed by Ambrose Philips: 'In summer shade, behind the cocking hay / What kind endearing words did she not say! / Her lap, with apron decked, she fondly spread / And strok'd my cheek, and lull'd my leaning head'

between their own experiences and Virgil's rural pursuits, and his description of an idyllic countryside would have had an obvious appeal. It would be interesting to know whether Lady Calverley had already decided on these particular illustrations when the overall design of the screen was discussed, or whether she and her husband were shown them at the pattern drawer on a visit to London.

The choice of prints and engravings increased throughout the eighteenth century, and established pattern drawers could offer many variations on pastoral and other popular themes, adapting them to suit their patrons' requirements. Lady Calverley's delightful design is proof of that 'wild kind of imagination' recommended in *The London Tradesman* of 1747 when describing the highly competitive business of pattern drawing. 'This required a fruitful Fancy, to invent new Whims to please the changeable Foible of the Ladies for whose use their Work is chiefly intended'.

Fanciful figures again create the impression of a rural masquerade in another entrancing set of wall panels made for Bryncinallt in North Wales by Prudence Trevor, daughter of Sir John Trevor, Master of the Rolls (see opposite). Contemporary with the Wallington embroideries, these reflect an enthusiasm for oriental and rustic themes, an enchanting blend of real and fantastic elements. The scale of the project – twelve panels 8ft (2.4m) tall and 5ft (1.5m) wide – suggests that Prudence Trevor, like Lady Calverley, was well supported by other needlewomen in the household, as was the case with some of the most ambitious sets of upholstered furniture.

Chair seats and backs were far less cumbersome to manage than carpets or hangings, and could also be shared out between family and friends, each of whom could stitch a variation on the overall theme, and enjoy the feeling that their contribution was pleasingly individual. *The Guardian* of 8 September 1713 mentions a Lady

Top left *The exotic trees and birds in Prudence Trevor's tent stitch panel recall the motifs in Indian chintzes and crewelwork, while the rounded hillocks renew the Elizabethan convention. Charmed by* *this fantasy, Belinda Downes draws a detail* (above)*, and then combines the motifs with others from Julia Calverley's cross stitch panels to create her own design* (top right)

Lizard who worked with her daughters to furnish a gallery with chairs and couches, 'and at the same time heard Doctor Tillotson's sermons twice over'. While a biblical theme would seem suitable for the pious Lizard ladies – Old and New Testament scenes do sometimes appear on early Georgian chairs, screens and pictures – pastoral, mythological, chinoiserie and floral subjects far outdid them in popularity.

Reading aloud and being read to while working was much appreciated, and the needlework often reflects the choice of books. The Stuart diet of sermons and devotional texts was lightened with readings from the classics, histories and carefully selected novels. Pastoral themes attracted British poets through much of the century, and new translations of Virgil and Ovid were immensely popular. Scenes such as the 'Rape of Europa', which Elizabethan embroiderers had displayed on valances, were now set in medallions garlanded with flowers on

William Welling's silhouette depicts stitching and reading aloud. Note the spectacles and basket for embroidery tools

Opposite *Fire-screen panel in coloured silks, c.1740. The design reflects the continuing vogue for chinoiserie*

sofas and chair backs. We can appreciate the continuing appeal of country scenes from Dr Johnson's praise of 'The Delights of Pastoral Poetry' in *The Rambler* on 21 July 1750 when he spoke of being transported to 'Elysian regions, where we meet with nothing but joy and plenty and contentment; where every gale whispers pleasure and every shade promises repose'.

As a traveller and guest up and down the country, Dr Johnson had ample opportunity to notice the needlework displayed in drawing rooms and bedrooms. In *The Idler* of 8 July 1758 he commented ironically on what he saw in a letter, echoing the complaints of Addison's despairing husband (see page 61). This correspondent's wife is likewise addicted to embroidery, and sets her unfortunate daughters an infinity of needlework tasks. As a result, 'We have twice as many fire screens as chimneys, and three flourished quilts for each bed. Half the rooms are adorned with a kind of *sutile* [stitched] *pictures* which imitate tapestry . . .'

These furnishings were shown off to guests with comments on the money she had saved. Exasperated, the husband tells his wife that her 'ornaments' are superfluous, would be better bought ready made, and are not worth the cost of the materials. Crossly, she retorts that she is starting on a dozen new chair covers. The husband has far more proper cause for complaint in her treatment of their daughters, who are shut up in a garret lit by a single window in the roof 'because work is best done at a skylight and because children are apt to lose time looking about them'. The girls stitch all morning on their own, continue under their mother's supervision through the afternoon, and 'grow up in total ignorance'.

The husband comments, 'Molly asked me, the other day, whether Ireland was in France and was ordered by her mother to mend her hem. Kitty knows not, at sixteen, the difference between a Protestant and a Papist, because she has been employed three years filling the side of a closet with a hanging that is to represent Cranmer in flames. And Dolly, my eldest girl, is now unable to read a chapter in the Bible having spent all her time, which other children pass at school, in working the interview between Solomon and the Queen of Sheba'.

Dr Johnson was not alone in commenting on the low standards of girls' education, and on the value of needlework in the curriculum. On 10 July 1748 Lady Mary Wortley Montagu summed up the situation: 'We are brought up in the grossest ignorance', she wrote sadly to her daughter, Lady Bute, regretting the fact that women with the same 'passion for learning' as herself had to hide their interests to avoid envy or ridicule. She considered some knowledge of history, geography and philosophy essential for getting the most out of life – yet she adds 'At the same time I recommend books, I neither exclude needlework or drawing. I think it is as scandalous for a woman not to know how to use her needle, as for a man not to know how to use a sword'.

Intrepid traveller, brilliant letter writer, she was also an accomplished needlewoman, and her opinions found a forceful champion in Samuel Richardson whose thrillingly romantic novels were avidly read by women of every age and class. Richardson shared Lady Mary's views on the importance of a balanced education for girls, including instruction in needlework. In *Pamela*, in 1741, he put them into the mouth of a servant girl, his heroine: 'I would indeed have a young lady brought up to her needle', Pamela writes, echoing Lady Mary's words, 'but I would not have *all* her time employed in samplers and learning to mark, and do those unnecessary things, which she will never, probably, be called upon to practice'.

Sampler making had become the accepted method of teaching girls to write and spell in the many boarding and institutional schools established during the eighteenth century. By 'learning to mark', Pamela meant stitching the alphabet and numerals, and possibly a row of crowns and coronets as well, which also provided useful practice for marking the quantities of linen used in a household of any size. Alphabets and numerals, together with a few improving words or stilted verses, had been commonplace

by the 1690s, squashed in between the close-packed rows of formalised patterns. But early in the eighteenth century these patterns, instead of being set one above another on a long narrow band, were rearranged as decorative borders framing much lengthier inscriptions on samplers that were square or rectangular in shape, and far more likely to be displayed as a picture on the wall than kept in a work-bag for reference.

Sampler making still taught children to be neat and diligent, but the emphasis was now more on instilling 'moral truths and duties' than learning virtuoso techniques. Schoolmistresses set their pupils to stitch out the *Lord's Prayer* or *Ten Commandments* as a centrepiece for their sampler, or culled improving texts from the

Above *Needlework in the schoolroom depicted in a print from* Curioser Spiegel, c.*1700*

Above *Late eighteenth-century sampler worked with a pastoral scene prettily framed in moss roses and violets*

Below *Variations in the popular bird-in-a-tree sampler motif*

*Waistcoat, c.1740,
embroidered with flowers
in brilliant crewel wools*

Psalms, or hymns from the *Divine Songs for Children* by the amiable non-conformist poet and preacher Dr Isaac Watts, whose lilting, sometimes entertaining verses were easily remembered and appealing to children. Whether or not this gave his young readers 'relish for virtue and religion', it was unlikely to develop their interest in embroidery, as in many cases only one stitch – satin or eyelets early in the century, then cross stitch – was used in the exercise. Perhaps Richardson's Pamela had this in

mind when she spoke of learning 'unnesessary things' lacking further use in needlework. As a 'low-born country girl' she had been taught fine needlework, not at school, but by her kind employer – as the novel opens she is working 'all hours' stitching linen and 'flowering a waistcoat' for 'Mr B', her dear departed mistress's importunate young son.

Though he never married, Watts spent much of his life with the family of his former parishioner Sr Thomas Abney, at Theobalds in Hertfordshire or in Stoke Newington. He watched the three Abney girls grow up, and must have seen how easily girls could be put off needlework if too much was expected of them. In his *Treatise of Education* (1725), he contrasts the ways two mothers educate their daughters; the first, Antigone, had been made to spend six hours a day at 'the labours of her needle'. Such excessive strictness determines her to allow her own children complete freedom – and so they are precocious and empty headed. The other mother Phronissa, steers a middle course between the 'severity of the last age and the wild licence of this', and teaches her girls 'all the plain and flowery arts of the needle', without making it a 'task or a toil'.

In *The Young Ladies' School of Arts* (1767) – a useful book explaining how to paint on silk and dye threads, with advice on japanning, gilding and other 'ornamental arts' – Mrs Hannah Robertson also warned against turning needlework into drudgery. She described how as soon as a girl can read, 'she has a piece of gauze put into her hand called a sampler . . . in which she finds so much difficulty that she takes a real disgust to school'. Most children were taught marking far too young, and Mrs Robertson found they learned 'better at ten or eleven than sooner'. She wanted girls to learn needlework 'for their own pleasure, or the ornament of their homes' or dress; training in embroidery might also prove invaluable 'in case of misfortunes happening in life'.

The most likely 'misfortune' was to fail to marry, or to become a widow without means. Spinsters and widows were only too familiar with the disadvantages of dependence on their male relations. Teaching was one of their few options, and in *The Governess* published in 1749, the author, Sarah Fielding, makes Mrs Teachum, owner of the 'Little Female Academy' in which the book is set, a widow who has lost her fortune and makes her living educating nine young ladies. One, Miss Jenny Peace, is aged fourteen, the rest are under twelve. Sarah had first-hand experience of boarding school, as she had been sent away at eight to Mrs Mary Rookes in the Close at Salisbury. There she learned embroidery and to 'read and write and talk french and Dance and be brought up like a gentlewoman'.

Like Isaac Watts' *Divine Songs* her book was an immediate success. She understood what appealed to children, and provided it in a new form. Treats and excitements outnumber punishments, as Sarah, like her brother Henry

Fielding, and her friend Samuel Richardson (who commented on the text before publication) all wished to 'mingle Instruction and Entertainment to make the latter seemingly the View, while the former is really the end'.

Good behaviour is rewarded on a red-letter day when Mrs Teachum's pupils first enjoy 'Plenty of Cream and Strawberries', and then see inside the local 'Nobleman's fine Seat' which was elegantly furnished with tapestries, paintings and 'the finest sorts of Needlework':

> When it came to the Needlework, Miss Jenny could not help smiling to see how everyone seemed most fixed in Attention upon that sort of Work, which she herself was employed in; and she saw in every face a secret Wish, that their own Piece of Work might be finished with equal Neatness and Perfection.

We can imagine that the girls admired chairs and stools in tent and cross stitch, and beds with counterpanes and valances in flat or corded quilting, or furnished with crewelwork hangings in flower and tree patterns that were lighter and prettier than those of the previous century, and stitched in brighter, gayer colours.

The fictional Mrs Teachum's affectionate understanding

In William Redmore Bigg's The Romps, *the girl holding her embroidery, and the work-bag and basket on the mantelpiece below the oval silk picture, make plain the importance of needlework in the school curriculum*

of her pupils is paralleled at the *real* Mrs Betsy Cumyn's school in Kensington Square. Here Hesther Thrale, close friend and correspondent of Dr Johnson, sent her daughters Susan and Sophy to be educated. Mrs Cumyns had been reduced 'to the necessity of keeping a school' as her 'shocking scoundrel of a husband' had absconded with all her money. She and Hesther were old friends, and Susan was entrusted to her in 1774 when she was only four.

Hesther had been taught needlework by her mother Mrs Salusbury, and they enjoyed stitching a carpet together of an evening. In 1772 her mother had given Dr Johnson a canvaswork chair made by Hesther 'when she was a good little girl and minded her book and needle'. Hesther expected her daughters to follow her example. She was an affectionate but demanding mother – her children were summoned with an ivory whistle. She recorded her childrens' progress in a *Family Book,* noting in 1775 that the five-year-old Susan had finished a shift for her sister all by herself. It exasperated her that Queenie, her eldest, despite her love of needlework was 'capricious and desirous to range from one thing to another without finishing any'. On 29 May 1777 Hesther praises 'Susan's Map Sampler' completed between the ages of six and seven as 'a good Specimen of her Work and Geography'.

Interest in geography was widespread as the blank spaces on the globe were gradually filled in with information supplied by travellers such as Commodore Anson, Captain Cook and Sir Joseph Banks. The notion of map samplers was seen as a topical way of reinforcing knowledge of geography, and imprinting the outlines of England and Wales, Europe and the two hemispheres on children's memories. Susan Thrale probably had her map drawn out on satin or linen by her teacher, but older children were encouraged to do this for themselves, often with wildly inaccurate results. The next part of the exercise was to fill in the names of countries, towns and villages, and this could lead to a further crop of errors.

It must have been a relief in the 1780s when maps

Below Chair cover, c.1760, depicting the orangery (1761) in the gardens at Gibside, Northumberland, embroidered by the eleven-year-old Eleanor Bowes. Later in life her interest in flowers led her to plant-hunting expeditions in the Cape in South Africa

Above Considerable confusion reigns in Anne Brown's map of England and Wales worked c.1795. Northumberland extends so far south that Exeter is north of York, and the Thames runs past the Isle of Wight! Wools on woollen tammy cloth

Above *Silk picture of Emma Hamilton with Admiral Nelson at Merton Park, possibly worked by her, c.1800. This charmingly informal scene contrasts with the more sombre memorial portraits adapted from popular engravings and worked in large numbers after Nelson's death in 1805*

Below *In the embroidery of William Redmore Bigg's* Harvest Girl (left) *speckling stitches recreate the effect of the stipple engraving* (right) *which inspired it*

specially printed on material began to appear, easy to follow in stem and cross stitch. Working the figure of Britannia or ships off the coast added a touch of variety, and framing the maps with be-ribboned posies made them more decorative – so much so that adults found them amusing to stitch as well. They were esteemed as gifts; on 11 June 1778 Mrs Thrale writes that 'Susan has worked a fine Map Sampler to send to my (Hesther's) aunt in Bath, in all shades, very elegant indeed. I warrant it will be enough admired'. Of her twelve children, only Queenie, Susan and Sophy grew to adulthood, and the *Family Book* records their illnesses and deaths in poignant detail. Most children grew up with the expectation that life was short and death imminent, and the sampler verses instilled resignation.

Both children and adults worked mourning pictures using silk on a painted silk ground, thus continuing the sorrowful theme of death common in neo-classical art. In a lively description of her first day as a pupil at Madame Latournelle's well run school at Reading Abbey in 1791, Mrs Sherwood writes of being received in 'a wainscotted parlour, hung round with chenille pieces representing tombs and weeping willows', which would have provided suitable proof of the pupils' attainments in needlework. These silk pictures were far less time-consuming than canvaswork furnishings, and interest had moved away from 'truly substantial tent work chairs and carpets'.

A lighter style of decoration had come into fashion, and the latest chairs and settees were covered in finely woven

Silk picture of a mother and children, c.1805. The curtains, carpet and wallpaper record the latest fashions in furnishing

tapestry from France, or in plain or unobtrusively pat-terned silks and velvets whose seductive sheen comple-mented the lustre of a satinwood or painted frame. Delicate silk pictures and pole screens with needlework panels fitted harmoniously in these pretty yet sophisti-cated schemes. The emphasis was once again on small scale embroideries whose only purpose was to be deco-rative and display the skill of the maker, an echo of the change of taste from canvas to raised work in the seven-teenth century. But the stitchery of the Georgian silk picture or 'satin sketch' was simple indeed compared to the intricacy of Stuart pictures; the patterns involved fewer figures and details, and the faces and part of the back-ground were painted on silk or satin. Provided the em-broiderer was practised in French knots and long and short and stem stitch, and had acquired the knack of using fluffy textured chenille to render the fleece of sheep and the foliage of trees, they could be worked quite swiftly and easily, as shown by the dates occasionally recorded

on the reverse of the picture.

Satin sketches became a craze lasting well into the nine-teenth century, and a tempting range of subjects were offered in kit form. Some embroiderers preferred to prepare the silk themselves, and thus displayed their aptitude in drawing and water-colour painting. These 'Polite accomplishments' rated equal to, or even higher than, needlework. Tuition in drawing helps to refine the eye and exercises in copying encouraged students to examine how artists achieved their effects. For a percep-tive embroiderer, study of the speckling in the new stipple engravings, and the use of shading in mezzotints could provide useful suggestions for stitchery. There is a good example in the *Harvest Girl* embroidered in a pointilliste technique inspired by the engraving of a painting by William Redmore Bigg. It can be seen in the drawing room of Fenton House in Hampstead, together with a col-lection of flower pictures beautifully shaded in silks, and two others depicting ladies in the splendidly elegant hats

Benjamin West depicts Queen Charlotte knotting, a favourite pastime throughout the eighteenth century. The shuttles and bags for holding the thread – one can be seen on her lap – were often presented as gifts and prettily ornamented, see page 94

of the 1790s, one watering her flowers, the other feeding chickens. Flowers provided inspiration for embroidery, and so did poultry, whose beguiling shapes and feather patterns were often interpreted in stitchery. Mrs Thrale kept ducks, chickens, turkeys, geese and peafowl at Streatham Park, and many ladies found it amusing to breed canaries, or to rear exotic-looking pheasants and other ornamental birds, and include them in their needlework.

New variations on country themes now became favourite subjects for silk pictures. There were updated versions of earlier pastorals with 'shepherds', 'reapers' and 'anglers' now dressed in the latest neo-classical fashions, and humbler peasant scenes adapted – and prettified – from the engravings of Frances Wheatley and George Morland. These depicted rural life, in 'tinsel trappings', as the poet George Crabbe wrote in *The Village* in 1783.

Despite their sentimental overtones, both artists' pictures were based on direct observation, with a genuine longing for rustic simplicity.

Sentiment was a selling point, and the suppliers of kits, knowing that many of their products would be bought for young embroiderers, provided a wide choice depicting children, either on their own, or happy in the company of their mothers and playmates. Parental love was another popular theme, reflecting the relaxed and affectionate attitude to children described by Sarah Fielding in *The Governess*.

A charming example of informal domesticity can be seen in Benjamin West's portrait of Queen Charlotte and the ten-year-old Princess Royal, painted in 1776. The young princess displays a delicately embroidered border, while her mother is knotting thread to make trimmings. Unlike silk embroidery and whitework, knotting did not demand close attention; it could be done by candlelight, and taken up while travelling in a coach or at social gatherings, where it gave a nice impression of diligence. The shuttles were enchantingly decorated, and in action they showed off the hands as elegantly as a fan. A pert letter from a 'pretty young thing of eighteen' to *The Spectator* (14 November 1712) suggested that gentlemen should take up knotting because 'it shows off a white hand and diamond ring to great advantage'.

According to Boswell, Dr Johnson tried 'once for his amusement' to knot, but found it beyond him. Had he persevered, he would soon have acquired the knack of flicking the shuttle rhythmically to form a series of knots in the thread, which could then be sewn down, either in outline or to fill in the motifs in a design. The size of the knots depended on the thickness of the thread wound in the shuttle. Tightly twisted wool or silk, linen and string could all be knotted, the finest trimmings resembling minute, loosely strung seed pearls, and the thickest chunky beads. These various types could be combined to create all sorts of interesting textural effects on furnishings.

The best known exponent was Mrs Mary Delany (1700-88), who recorded her enthusiasm for knotting and many different methods of embroidery in her voluminous correspondence, edited in the 1860s by her great grand niece Lady Llanover. Lady Llanover tells us that Mrs Delany and her sister Anne Dewes used their shuttles for relaxation, and that Mrs Delany left quantities of knotted trimmings: 'the produce of tea-table leisure hours'. Mrs Delany appreciated knotting for its versatility and hard-wearing qualities. On 27 October 1750, she wrote to her sister promising to produce some with the largest knots, which she called 'sugar plums', once she had finished 'a plain fringe I am knotting to trim a new blue and white linen bed I have just put up'. Blue, 'either dark and bright or sky blue' was her favourite colour for furnishing. For a set of chairs at Delville, her much loved home near Dublin, she chose brilliant blue linen, ornamented with a design of ribbon-tied swags of leaves and husks, most inventively rendered in five different types of knotting.

When she was asked by Queen Charlotte to design a set of chair covers, Mrs Delany again chose her favourite blue ground, but instead of knotting, recommended appliqué in a leaf pattern in shades of brown. She had first met Queen Charlotte in 1776 at Bulstrode, the home of her great friend the Duchess of Portland, and she was soon on affectionate terms with the entire royal family, a uniquely privileged position which she enjoyed to the end of her life. On a later visit to Bulstrode on 12 August 1778, 'the Queen sat down and called me to talk about the chenille work, praising it much more than it deserved, but with a politeness that could not fail of giving pleasure'. Mrs Delany often used 'a very peculiar worsted chenille', and this would have intrigued Queen Charlotte, as she was interested in every aspect of needlework.

A set of chairs in the Queen's rooms at the Upper Lodge

The sophisticated textural effect of knotting is shown in this detail of a hanging made by Princess Amelia, an expert needlewoman, daughter of George II

Above *Mrs Delany's silhouette depicts knotting and reading aloud*

Right The Ladies New Memorandum Book *of 1789 records Queen Charlotte's visit to Mrs Wright's embroidery school*

at Windsor was 'in knotted silk floss of different shades sewn to imitate natural flowers'. Describing the 'elegant simplicity' and lightness of the decoration in her apartments, Mary Hamilton notes that 'Her Majesty has done a great deal of the knotting herself'. We get another delightfully informal glimpse of Queen Charlotte engaged in needlework in the cottage in Richmond Gardens (now Kew), while George III read aloud from Shakespeare (see *Royal Friendships* by C. Gearey, 1898).

Queen Charlotte encouraged her daughters' artistic interests, and saw that they were well grounded in needlework by Mademoiselle Montmollin, their Swiss governess, who also taught them history and how to net purses. The value the Queen placed in needlework instruction extended beyond her daughters, and led her to set up a small school – established in Great Newport Street in London – where girls of limited means but good family were taught embroidery by Mrs Phoebe Wright and her niece Nancy Pawsey. One of the most important projects was a set of furnishings for the Queen's bed, whose delicate embroidery of flowers can still be admired at Hampton Court Palace. Here Queen Charlotte's enthusiasms came together: she was extremely interested in botany and horticulture, and the design included many current flower favourites exquisitely shaded in long and short stitch in coloured silks on lilac satin. Queen Charlotte must therefore have followed the project's progress with keen interest.

Another embroiderer whose expertise attracted Queen Charlotte's attention was the vivacious Mrs Mary Knowles (1733-1802), described by Boswell as 'the ingenious Quaker Lady'. Mrs Knowles specialised in 'needlepainting', in which straight stitches were closely worked to reproduce the brushmarks of an artist working in oils. Her copies of famous paintings so impressed Queen Charlotte that she commissioned her to recreate Zoffany's portrait of George III in woolwork. It must be remembered that no

Opposite *Toronds*
silhouette of the Parminter
family shows a lady using
a netting box (see page 94)

Above *Mrs Knowles' self-*
portrait in wools depicts
her at work on her needle-
painting of George III.

Both needlepaintings can
be seen at Kew Palace

slur was attached to imitating paintings at the time. Copying was an established method of learning to draw; many enthusiasts, Mrs Delany among them, enjoyed copying great paintings and having their versions admired. In addition, collecting old master paintings and engravings and commissioning portraits of the family was much in vogue.

'The collection in the house is curious', wrote the traveller and farming expert Arthur Young when, on a tour of north-east England in 1771, he visited Rokeby Park in County Durham where he saw works by Poussin, Zucarelli and Salvator Rosa. This rich collection provided inspiration for the remarkable needlepaintings worked by Anne Morritt (1726-97), who spent much of her life at Rokeby. Young had seen examples of her work at York, and was astonished at her skill in copying fine paintings

'with a grace, a brilliancy and an elegance superior to the originals'; she was 'a lady of most surprizing (*sic*) genius'.

At the age of twelve Anne Morritt was already adept at long and short stitch, and by the time she was thirty she had developed her own original style. Her 'brilliancy' lay in freely interpreting rather than slavishly copying, using

Above *Anne Morritt selected details from a large bird picture by Marmaduke Craddock (1660-1716) for a series of needlepaintings. Two delectable robins and a family of ducks as well as this spirited group are preserved together with the painting at Rokeby*

Opposite *The textural contrast of fur and foliage is inventively rendered in wools in Mrs Thomas Butts' needlepainting*

straight stitches obviously worked at speed and with great verve. She could convey the bloom on a grape or sheen on a pheasant's plumage – a feeling for texture that led her to isolate details from large paintings as subjects for her embroidery.

Mrs Knowles and Miss Morritt were fine draughtswomen as well as expert embroiderers, but neither ever enjoyed the good fortune of Mrs Thomas Butts in having a great artist design specifically for them. Mrs Butts was a friend and patron of William Blake at the turn of the century, and he drew two designs for her, one of hares, the other of dead game. Mrs Butts' striking interpretation of the hares shows her to have been an imaginative as well as an accomplished needlewoman. As a frequent visitor to the house, Blake would have seen her work and appreciated her skill, making it possible for that rare and ideal situation in which (as Lewis F. Day put it in *Art in Needlework*, 1900) 'designer and worker are entirely in sympathy, when the designer knows exactly what the worker can do with her materials, and when the worker not only understands what the designer meant, but feels with him'.

A delightful variant on needlepainting, using silks rather than wools to create convincing *trompe l'oeil* effects, can be seen at Arbury Hall in Warwickshire, where Sophia Conyers, first wife of Sir Roger Newdigate, worked the covers for a set of stools. It is said that her husband, used to seeing her possessions left lying about the house, suggested that she make them the subject of her designs. We should be grateful to him, as Sophia's covers bring alive her pastimes and interests in a uniquely pleasing and original manner. On one stool cover we see her ribbon-tied straw hat tossed down by a book; on another, an almanac for 1757 with a length of lace, a hank of silk and three pieces of card on which thread had been wound; while a third shows her fan half open over a hussif and lace fichu. Her knotting shuttle, threads and work-bag lie together suggesting that, like Mrs Delany, she had more than one project in hand at a time. Indeed they suggest work in progress far more eloquently than the pretty cane baskets that appear in a number of Arthur Devis' portraits, neatly placed by the sitter's hand, so that she can toy with a silver thimble or dainty pair of scissors. The suspicious similarity of the baskets suggests that Devis, who sometimes posed his prosperous bourgeois patrons in grander settings than they enjoyed at home, kept one as a prop to

Stool cover, one of seven, worked in silks by Sophia Conyers

flatter his clients' aspirations of elegance and gentility.

Though everyday tools could still be bought from pedlars and at fairs, the prettiest scissors, needlecases and shuttles came from the smart London 'toy shops', like Deards in Pall Mall. Toy shops specialised, not in children's playthings, but in desirable small gifts for adults, made in materials such as gold, silver, tortoiseshell and painted enamel. As well as purely decorative

'Baubles', there were 'Useful Curiosities', among them the latest writing and needlework novelties, such as chatelaines which served the purpose of a handbag, and enabled one to carry round a pencil, *aide mémoire*, spectacle case and selection of small tools hung on delicate chains, attached to a clasp at the waist.

Chatelaines were expensive, and could be cumbersome, and so many needlewomen preferred to embroider

Paddy Killer's drawing of a work-basket, unrolled hussif, thimbles, *folding scissors and étui are arranged as in a portrait by Arthur Devis. Spectacles with ring-end side pieces were first made in the 1740s*

themselves a folding case or hussif with compartments for the most used items. A very superior and compact version, described as a white satin 'letter case' ornamented with spangles, was given to Mrs Delany by Queen Charlotte on 15 December 1781. It was lined with pink satin and contained 'sizsars, pencle, rule, compass and bodkin' in gold and mother of pearl, and a most affectionate note in the Queen's own hand.

Such beautifully presented sets were often imported from Paris. Elaborately carved mother-of-pearl handles were a speciality of the French craftsmen, but tended to be fragile – a serious defect where scissors and bodkins were concerned. Mrs Delany must have been a connoisseur of reliable well-made scissors, and might well have found an *étui* or case containing a pair of ingeniously designed all steel scissors with folding handles the most practical for her needs. In 1772 when she was seventy-two, she began making her remarkable cut paper flowers that demanded scissors of razor sharpness to achieve the closely observed details at which she excelled.

Mrs Delany's interest in handwork began as a child, encouraged first by her mother, Mrs Granville, who was accomplished in needlework and spinning, and then by Mademoiselle Puelle, a French refugee who ran a small school in London. There Mary practised plain sewing, learned decorative stitches and how to cut silhouettes. These skills were to stand her in good stead when at seventeen, due to a disastrous change in the family's fortunes, she sadly consented to marry Alexander Pendarves, a Cornish landowner over forty years her senior with whom she had nothing in common. Immured with a husband she found 'disgusting rather than engaging' in the bleak surroundings of Roscrow Castle near Falmouth, it must have been a relief to immerse herself in 'a variety of works' as she sat at the bedside of the gout-ridden and cantankerous Mr Pendarves.

Released from this unhappy marriage by his death in 1724, she was free to follow her own pursuits, and enjoy the musical and social scene in London. She studied the 'abundance of embroidery' worn at court on grand occasions, and in her letters to her sister Anne she described the most eye-catching outfits in vivid detail, commenting wittily on the levels of taste exhibited by the wearers. On 4 March 1729, she was at Queen Caroline's birthday celebration. 'I dressed myself in my best array', she tells Anne excitedly, 'and made a tearing show' – contrived no doubt by her own hands. The exquisite embroidery of flowers on the black silk court dress she worked for herself in the

This detail of oriental poppies on Mrs Delany's court dress shows her exceptional skill at delineating botanically accurate flowers in long and short stitch in twisted silks

1750s testifies to her taste, sophisticated sense of design and mastery of long and short stitch.

When in 1743 she married Dr Patrick Delany, one of the delights of her life at Delville was the constant interest her husband showed in all her projects:

> His approving of my works, and encouraging me to go on, keep up my relish to them, and make them more delightful to me than assemblies, plays, or an opera would be without he shared them with me. *Eager* as I am in all my pursuits, I am *easily checked and the least disapprobation or snap,* from the person I wish to oblige, in thought, word or deed would soon give me a distaste to what was delightful to me before!

How different from Samuel Pepys' snappish comments at his wife's attempts at embroidery!

Mrs Delany's 'pursuits' were remarkable in their variety. In needlework she was ever eager to try out a new method or materials, though always with a definite purpose in view. She stitched feathers for an unusual tippet, and experimented with chintz both as a ground and for appliqué. The gentle rhythms of cross stitch were soothing, and cross stitch covered the ground quickly. We can picture her on a late November evening that same year, seated by the fire with her friend Mrs Letty Bushe 'finishing a carpet in double cross stitch to go round my bed'. Filling in the background was ideal 'candlelight work', a satisfying occupation for 'leisure moments'. The fine work of shading in tent stitch or long and short stitch demanded daylight, and she would have agreed with another friend, Mrs Boscawen, when in 1774 the latter wrote that it was 'curious to see my Ly Leicester work at a tent stitch frame every night by one candle that she sets upon it, and no spectacles. It is a carpet that she works in shades – tent stitch'.

After Dr Delany's death in 1768, Mrs Delany returned to England, spending months each year staying at Bulstrode with her closest friend, the Dowager Duchess of Portland. These visits provided just the stimulus she needed to embark on new projects. The two ladies were passionately interested in botany and horticulture, and the park and gardens at Bulstrode were idyllic in summer. Early each morning Mrs Delany would set off to visit the menagerie and enjoy the exotic birds and animals in the Duchess' collection. Marvelling at the 'dazzling and varied plumage' of the birds, she made sketches which she later used as subjects for the embroidery of a set of chairs for her friend: 'I have worked Caton (one of the parrots) in the back of one of the chenille chairs I am doing for the Duchess, in the midst of *purple astres* (asters) which sets off his golden plumage to admiration. I see much wanting in working it, but my partial friend is satisfied and that's enough'.

A parrot, shaded in worsteds by Caroline Campbell, Lady Ailesbury, suggests how Caton may have looked. This was one of twenty-two needlepaintings which Mrs Lybbe Powys noted in 1784 in the drawing room of Park Place, Lady Ailesbury's home near Henley-on-Thames.

White tiffany three-cornered handkerchief embroidered by Mrs Delany with be-ribboned flowers

A parrot (above) *and a favourite dog* (below) *recorded in worsted in*

Lady Ailesbury's needlepaintings

Embroidery design by Mrs Delany

Horace Walpole, elegant letter writer and wit, was a close friend of Lady Ailesbury and an admirer of her work, calling her 'a very great Mistress of the Art of Needlework who surpassed the Pictures she copied'. In a letter written to her husband, General Conway, he described his delight when she sent him 'the most beautiful of all her pictures', a landscape after Van Uden. He corresponded with her for over twenty years, and, on 3 October 1773, wrote her a particularly entertaining letter telling her how he had amused himself at church rearranging the text of the collect taken from the fourth chapter of St Mark, which begins (verse 3) 'Behold there came a Sower to sow' so that it fitted her needlepaintings. Like many of her contemporaries, Lady Ailesbury had chosen ornamental poultry as one of her subjects (a 'piece of fowls', inspired perhaps by the guinea fowl she kept at Park Place, was exhibited at the Society of Artists in 1768), so Walpole played with the next verse until it read 'And it came to pass, as She sow'd, some stitches fell on a *Farm yard,* and the Fowls of the Air came and dwelt therein . . . and so on through eight more verses which ingeniously introduced the flowers, fruit and dogs she had also embroidered.

On his visits to country houses, Walpole would have been familiar with the friendly clutter of books and needlework in progress so vividly described in Mrs

Reynold's portrait shows Lady Horatia Waldegrave working chain stitch with a hook on muslin held firmly by the strap of her tambour frame. Note the pretty work-bag on the table

Below *Tambourwork diagram showing how the hook picks up loops of thread to form a continuous chain*

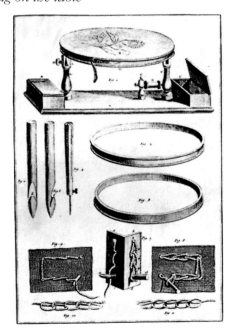

One lady knots while another works flower sprigs on a tambour frame in P.M. Tomkins' engraving (1789) of H.W. Bunbury's Morning Employment

Delany's letters. At least three of his female correspondents were needlewomen. He bought three knotting bags for Lady Hervey in Paris, and wore a waistcoat tamboured for him by Lady Ossory. Tambourwork was all the rage in the 1780s, and in the portrait of his much loved great nieces, the Ladies Waldegrave, painted for him by Sir Joshua Reynolds in 1780, the youngest, Lady Horatia, is depicted with her tambour hook poised above the large round tambour frame from which this method of working chain stitch takes its name. Lady Maria sits opposite her holding a skein of silk which Lady Laura, the eldest, winds on to a card.

Tambourwork suited the mood of the moment, as it could be worked easily and at great speed to create the

A silhouette of the architect James Essex and family. His daughter is tambouring on a rectangular frame while his wife feeds a pet squirrel

light, delicate ornament then so much in vogue. The flowing patterns looked stylish on coloured materials, and especially beguiling on white muslin made up in the soft pretty styles worn by the Ladies Waldegrave. It is a world away from the intricate stitchery of Dresden work, in which the threads of gossamer-fine muslin were pulled together to form patterns resembling the most expensive lace, but, as the delicate sprays on the muslin stretched on Lady Horatia's frame show, it was the ideal method to achieve the simple, but refined effects that were then the height of fashion.

There was no difficulty in finding suitable designs, as 'the most elegant patterns for tambour or every kind of embroidery' were a special feature in periodicals like the *Lady's Magazine* which first appeared in 1770. Magazines targeting an exclusively feminine readership had all the charm of novelty, and the inclusion of ready-to-use patterns was a shrewd inducement to buy them regularly. The stories, recipes and patterns were 'calculated for your amusement', and undoubtedly delighted the purchasers, as they removed almost all the pull-out patterns from the copies that survive in libraries today.

The most appealing were lent to friends, and, like the pricked designs in sixteenth and seventeenth-century pattern books, quickly disintegrated. Some favourites however were providently preserved in special books or albums, as a personal collection, by copying either the pattern itself or the worked design. Exchanging patterns

was especially important in the remoter parts of the country where news of the latest fashions travelled slowly. Nancy, niece of Parson James Woodforde of diary fame, kept a detailed journal during 1792 in which she describes the custom. Like many of her contemporaries Nancy had her gowns made professionally, but enjoyed embroidering accessories for herself. She noted the loan of a muslin petticoat and several handkerchief patterns, one of which she copied and worked in three days for her friend Mrs Custance. These could have been pocket handkerchiefs, but were more likely to have been large squares of silk or muslin to tuck becomingly into the bodice of a high-waisted gown.

Late in the century there was a fashion for tambouring or working the entire fabric for a gown. This was 'a very great undertaking' as Maria Holroyd remarked in 1790, when she started on a 'Gown in Spots', and we feel for her when she adds 'I hope the Fashions will have the complaisance to wait for me and that spotted Muslins will not go out'. Provided that she did not succumb to the boredom of stitching endless spots in French knots or satin stitch, her hopes were likely to be confirmed. After decades of tight corseting the appeal of soft 'sewed muslins', so pleasant and comfortable to wear, and so charmingly informal in comparison to the stiff silks and heavy satins, brocades and velvets of yesteryear ensured their popularity – the height of fashion at the end of the century, they remained in favour throughout the Regency.

'Early nineteenth-century whitework patterns traced from the manuscript book of Theophania Fairfax, reproduced in The Embroideress *(1927)*

'A new fancy pattern for working in colours' from the Lady's Magazine, *1792*

Regency
Interlude

No one can be really esteemed accomplished, who does not greatly surpass what is usually met with.
Pride and Prejudice, Jane Austen, 1813

If Mrs Delany's letters take us into the Georgian embroiderer's world in a most pleasurable and intimate manner, Jane Austen's novels (published between 1811 and 1818) are rewarding in providing glimpses of Regency ladies at work. Though her references to needlework are less detailed and less frequent than Mrs Delany's, they are nonetheless extremely revealing. In *Mansfield Park* we can picture Lady Bertram stitching endlessly, if absent-mindedly, with her pug beside her and her niece Fanny Price hovering in attendance, ready to put right the mistakes she is sure to make. Jane Austen's description of Lady Bertram as 'a woman who spent her time sitting nicely dressed on a sofa doing some long piece of needlework of little use and no beauty' could have been applied to many of her contemporaries.

Needlework was still part of a 'polite education', and the female characters in her novels often spent time each day on 'work', but its value as an accomplishment was no longer taken for granted. 'No one can be really esteemed accomplished, who does not greatly surpass what is usually met with', states Miss Bingley, during an animated discussion on the meaning of the word in *Pride and Prejudice*. She lists music, singing, drawing and modern languages as indispensable, but makes no mention of needlework, whereas her affable brother Charles finds all the young ladies of his acquaintance accomplished on the grounds that they can 'paint tables, cover screens and net

Morning dress for 1814 from Ackermann's Repository of Arts. *Rudolph Ackermann was a leading print-seller and supplier of embroidery equipment*

Opposite *Each fashion plate in* Costume Parisien *(1817) was accompanied by patterns for handkerchiefs, flounces and borders*

Above *Jane Austen's muslin scarf, a handkerchief with Cassandra's initials, and a needlecase made for her niece, arranged on the coverlet* she pieced together with her mother and Cassandra. This detail shows how ingeniously small patches of spotted cotton were fitted into the border

Coins de Mouchoir de Poche.

purses'. But for Mr Darcy, this is merely proof of the sadly limited extent of their talents, taste and education.

Jane Austen is a reliable commentator on the embroidery of her time, being both a sharp-eyed observer of society and an expert needlewoman with a keen interest in dress. In her correspondence with her sister Cassandra she often mentions clothes and needlework, and there are echoes of Mrs Delany's affectionate dialogue with her sister Anne (see page 77) in a letter written in December 1808: 'I wish I *could* help you in your needlework. I have two hands and a new thimble that lead a very idle life.'

Some of her embroidery is preserved at Chawton in Hampshire, where she lived from 1808 till shortly before her death in 1817, and we are therefore able to see her accomplished stitchery for ourselves. There is a muslin scarf delicately worked with a trellis border in white on white, and a lawn handkerchief, also in white, with a different motif in each corner embroidered for her sister Cassandra in satin stitch – charming examples of the fashion for 'sewed muslins' embellished with whitework. 'A woman can never be too fine while she is all in white', says Edmund to his cousin Fanny in *Mansfield Park,* 'Your gown is very pretty, I like the glossy spots'. The glossy effect would have been achieved in meticulously even satin stitch in which Jane Austen excelled. By her own admission she was proud of her neatness, and according to her nephew, James Edward Austen-Leigh, she was exceptionally deft with her fingers. In the *Memoir* he wrote in 1871, Austen-Leigh tells us 'Her needlework both plain and ornamental was excellent, and she might have put a

Motifs for caps and a border from Costume Parisien, *1817*

Below *Needlework, reading and writing depicted at Brathay Hall in 1829 in a watercolour of his family by John Harden*

sewing machine to shame. She was considered especially great in satin stitch. She spent much time in this occupation, and some of her merriest talk was over clothes which she and her companions were making, sometimes for themselves and sometimes for the poor'.

His affectionate word picture and many of the scenes in her novels are brought magically to life and, as it were, confirmed in the intimate watercolours and drawings John Harden made of his family and friends at work at Brathay Hall, the Harden home near Lake Windermere. As at Chawton, reading, writing, music and needlework often took place in the same room, and we can almost hear the snip of scissors and murmur of conversation. His drawings show how people still made do with one or two candles and firelight in the evenings, repositioning tables and chairs to make the best use of light and warmth.

Jane Austen was interested in knotting, a favourite candlelight occupation, and she also enjoyed patchwork – which demanded the deftness and neatness which were her forte. At Chawton we can still admire the coverlet she made with her mother and Cassandra around 1811 when patchwork was all the rage. Patchwork was already well known in the 1720s when Jane Barker entitled her miscellany of short stories *A Patchwork Screen for Ladies* (1722), and Swift described the outfit made by the Lilliputian tailors for his hero in *Gulliver's Travels* (1726) as looking 'like the patchwork made by the ladies of England', but it only became a craze towards the end of the century. As so often happens it was boosted by the availability of new materials – in this case the wealth of gaily-patterned inexpensive cottons, which wore well and retained their bright colours when washed.

Late eighteenth-century printwork picture recording Burghley House, Lincolnshire, finely worked in hair in speckling and straight stitches

The decorative possibilities of 'sewing small pieces of different colours interchangeably together' – to quote Dr Johnson's definition – were quickly grasped, and the fun of pattern-making could begin. Like many Regency coverlets, the Austen ladies' work is most carefully planned and beautifully executed. They chose diamond shapes in three sizes, the smallest pieced as a wide border, the medium size outlined in patches of spotted cotton, and the largest in the centre – a single diamond cut from a flower basket chintz.

Pictorial embroidery in both silks and worsteds was still popular, especially print-style landscapes (in imitation of engravings) worked in shades of grey and black silk, or occasionally hair. The Duchess of Gloucester, sister-in-law of George III and mother of the Waldegrave sisters, embroidered a view of distant hills and trees with cattle, sheep and figures in the foreground, using her own and her six children's hair to provide different tints of brown, gold and auburn.

In *Sense and Sensibility,* Jane Austen mentions a landscape in silks made by Charlotte Palmer which hung over the mantelpiece in her apartment 'in proof of her having spent seven years at a great school to some effect'. Jane herself had attended Kendrick School in Reading, close to the establishment run by Madame Latournelle (see page 74), and she would have been familiar with the schoolmistresses' eagerness to display proof of their pupils' skills.

Boarding schools were springing up everywhere. Whereas they had formerly been the exclusive preserve of the nobility and gentry, now many of them were welcoming the daughters of wealthy farmers and tradesmen, determined to see their offspring rise in the world. Gillray's cartoon, drawn three years before *Sense and Sensibility* was published, ridicules the aspirations of the rich and rapidly growing middle classes in the person of Farmer Giles, delightedly showing off his daughter Betty's newly acquired 'accomplishments' to the neighbours. Her piano playing, and the sampler and silk picture on the wall are proof positive of her transformation into a gentlewoman.

This cartoon might have been drawn to illustrate the moral tale of *The Two Wealthy Farmers* (printed in Cheap Repository Tracts, *c*.1795-97) by the educationalist Hannah More. This tells of Farmer Bragwell and his wife, who, mistakenly thinking that gentility consists in being 'rich and idle', send their two daughters to school to 'set them above the neighbours'. They return with 'vanity grafted onto their native ignorance', unwilling to help either of their parents, and interested only in experiencing 'romance'. They were 'too polite to be of any use', and Mrs Bragwell's only comfort lay in 'observing how her parlour was set about with their filigree and flowers, their embroidery and cut paper'. Despite these 'ornamental' accomplishments, they were never taught plain sewing at school – an omission which the eldest daughter, Polly, regrets when she is left destitute by her impostor of a

A cow features in Betty Giles' needlework, proudly displayed in Gillray's cartoon of 1808

husband, and with a child to support. Plain sewing might have secured her a job as a nursery maid, and it is only the 'thought of the fine netting she used to make for trimmings' that saves her from starvation. She procures some twine and makes cabbage and fishing nets to sell.

Yet Farmer Bragwell, still deluded by notions of gentility, is outraged, and instead of praising her initiative, he rebukes her for sinking to such a 'mean trade' – little knowing that it was a pastime favoured not only by the gentry, but by such aristocratic ladies as the Duchess of Portland, who, according to Mrs Delany, made fine meshed nets to keep the birds from her cherries.

This was at Bulstrode in 1783, and at a wedding three years later, Mrs Delany noted an original use of netting – forming a waistcoat, made 'for the groom by his bride'. Netting appealed to men as well as women. In his long poem *The Task*, written in 1784, William Cowper recommends the making of 'bird alluring nets' as a fireside occupation, and Jane Austen writes of her nephews amusing themselves of an evening with making rabbit nets.

These utilitarian nets were coarse indeed, compared with accessories and trimmings of handmade net embellished with darned decoration in imitation of lace, but the *method*, using a special needle or shuttle to loop and twist the thread into mesh was the same. Henry Moser's

soon will the awful hour appear
When i must quit my dwelling here
These active limbs to worms a prey
In the cold grave must waste away

Elizabeth Fagg
Aged 9 Years

Above *A cow features prominently in Elizabeth Fagg's sampler. The house and verse are typical of early nineteenth-century samplers*

Below left *Instruction in needlework from* The Thimble Restored, *1825*

Below right The Industrious Cottager *making cabbage nets in an engraving after Frances Wheatley*

The THIMBLE RESTORED.

Sewing Party shows a fashionable lady netting a purse, the 'accomplishment' scorned by Mr Darcy in *Pride and Prejudice*. Before the invention of metal-framed purses later in the century, the netted variety were not only pretty, but practical for keeping coins safe, and the large numbers that have survived testify to the truth of Mr Bingley's statement that the young ladies of his acquaintance 'all net purses'.

Special boxes could be bought for keeping the netting tools and threads, some fitted with a small roller pierced with holes to secure the foundation loop and keep the netting taut while working. Like the tools for knotting and tambourwork, they were frequently offered as gifts and prettily decorated.

Fanny Price was given several by her cousins at Mansfield Park, indeed 'the table between the windows was covered with work-boxes and netting boxes . . . and she grew bewildered as to the amount of debt which all these kind remembrances produced'. While beautifully fitted boxes became increasingly popular, a basket or bag

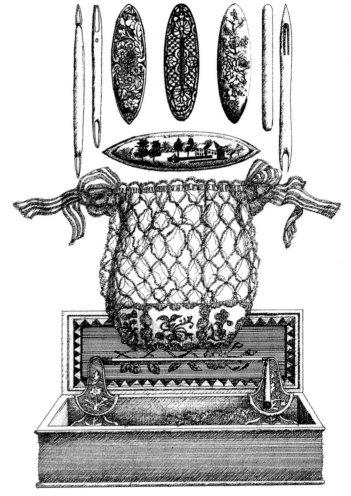

Above *Spotted muslin gown with a netted upper robe from* The Lady's Monthly Museum, *1800*

Below *Even the chairs are embellished with a knotted fringe in Henry Moses'* Sewing Party *from his* Designs for Modern Costume, *1812*

Above *Prettily decorated knotting shuttles, a work-bag and netting tools – needles, a gauge and special box with a roller to which the foundation loop was attached when working (see page 78)*

Opposite *An anonymous watercolour c.1815, depicts Anne Trump Furnell and her daughter Lydia stitching. The needlework box is preserved at the Quaker Friends' School at Ackworth, West Yorkshire, founded in 1797, together with samplers made by them and by pupils at the school*

was still useful for keeping favourite tools together. James Austen-Leigh mentions a work-box and netting case on the table at Chawton, and he also describes a 'curious specimen' of his aunt's needlework made for his mother, Jane Austen's sister-in-law:

'In a very small bag is deposited a little, rolled up housewife, furnished with miniken needles and fine thread. In the housewife is a tiny pocket, and in the pocket is enclosed a slip of paper, on which, written as with a crow quill, are these lines:

> This little bag, I hope, will prove
> To be not vainly made;
> For should you thread and needles want,
> It will afford you aid.
>
> And, as we are about to part,
> 'Twill serve another end:
> For, when you look upon this bag,
> You'll recollect your friend.

It is the kind of article that some benevolent fairy might be supposed to give as a reward to a diligent little girl. The whole is of flowered silk, and having never been used and carefully preserved, it is as fresh and bright as when it was first made some seventy years ago; and shows that the same hand which painted so exquisitely with the pen could work as delicately with the needle'.

Folding housewifes or hussifs had been sold in Georgian toy shops, but some of the most endearing examples were made at home, recalling Jane Austen's in the fairy-like daintiness of their decoration. 'Minikin' is an apt word to describe the exceptionally fine needles available at the turn of the century. The needlemakers had developed a range that were ideal for print work (see page 91), with eyes tiny enough to take the thinnest strand of hair. An added refinement was that the needles were now presented in rust-proof packets which could be arranged in specially made boxes with sloping lids.

It was even easier to select the right size from the flannel pages of needlebook, a useful alternative to a cylindrical case. Jane Austen made one for her niece Louisa, delicately painting the card cover, and sending it with a note inscribed 'with Aunt Jane's love'. I feel that, with her enthusiasm for stitchery, she would have undoubtedly selected the needles with care. Exactly the right eye must be chosen for the thread used in satin stitch if the proper gloss is to be achieved, and fairly short needles that combine fineness with strength are best suited to the close seaming essential for patchwork.

Patchwork and appliqué both demand the sharpest scissors, and we can imagine that the Austen ladies kept one or more pairs specially for cutting the paper shapes,

Muslin gown with Greek-inspired decoration to complement a fashionable interior drawn by Henry Moses. Note the scissors and sewing basket on the table

as this easily blunts the blades, and that they reserved others for the material. The sharp points easily poke through a work-bag, and most pairs were sold with a sheath. At a tense moment in *Sense and Sensibility,* when Edward Ferrers has to reveal his brother's marriage to Lucy Steele, he 'took up a pair of scissors . . . spoiling both them and their sheath by cutting the latter to pieces as he spoke'. Whether the scissors were ruined beyond repair would have depended on the toughness of the leather used in making the sheath. Scissors with blades strong and sharp enough to cut firm, closely-woven woollen materials such as broadcloth and felt into the most delicate flower petals were available at the time, as we may see from the felt appliqué pictures and furnishings made by Georgian and Regency needlewomen.

Vases and baskets of fruit were favourite subjects for pictures set in deep frames, specially made to show off three-dimensional effects reminiscent of stumpwork, but achieved with far less time and effort. In many of these designs, the similarity of the flowers suggests that, as with

Appliqué picture admired by Miss Jekyll

the silk pictures, some appliqué versions were available as kits, with the felt ready cut out. Writing on eighteenth-century needlework flower pictures in *Some English Gardens* in 1904, Gertrude Jekyll commented that 'though sometimes a drawing was made, many of them look as if they were worked direct from the flowers'. As in Dutch flower paintings, spring, summer and autumn flowers often appear together, and Miss Jekyll suggests that the needlewomen started on the spring varieties and then continued with those of summer as they bloomed, to create ' a jumble of seasons but a concord of pretty things . . . all done with a sweetness, a directness of intention and absence of strain and affectation, that gives them a singular charm'.

Her words perfectly describe a remarkable wall hanging in coloured wool appliqué made by Magdalene, daughter of William Blair of Blair, who married Sir William Maxwell, third Baronet of Monreith in Wigtownshire. The design is typical of mid-eighteenth-century coverlets, with a central basket of flowers and cornucopias in the corners linked by garlands looped up with tasselled bows, but the wide choice of flowers and many different types of wool, velvet and felt used in the appliqué are particularly interesting. According to her descendant, Sir Herbert Maxwell, the flowers record in detail those grown in the walled garden of Myrton Castle, the family home before they moved to Monreith – where the hanging may still be seen.

In *Old West Surrey* (1904), Miss Jekyll describes a more humble version of felt appliqué, a basket with a 'strikingly lifelike auricula', pansies and strawberries made from odd scraps of material at the end of the eighteenth century. 'It has the attraction of a thing that is perfectly sincere, showing the worker's delight in the things portrayed, and in the actual doing of the pretty whimsical little picture'. In about 1920, when her eyes were too poor for fine stitchery, Miss Jekyll made her own basket of strawberries in felt appliqué, drawing inspiration as we might do, from this early form of collage.

The central basket of flowers in the Monreith hanging

– 5 –

The Victorian Embroiderer

We should have nothing in our houses, which we did not either know to be useful or believe to be beautiful.

'The Beauty of Life' lecture, William Morris, 1880

In John Everett Millais' painting *Mariana*, the solitary maiden stands by her embroidery frame waiting for her knight's return to the moated grange. Inspired by Tennyson's poem 'Mariana', with its haunting refrain: 'I am aweary, aweary, I wish that I were dead', the painting brought Mariana's sentiments vividly to life. The stitchery of flowers that had occupied the hours of waiting appears all but complete, a detail pointing to the hopelessness of her situation, and one that would have been instantly picked up by many of the ladies who saw the picture when it was first exhibited in May 1851 at the Royal Academy in London.

Steeped in the romance of Tennyson's poetry, Sir Walter Scott's stirring historical novels, and a rich flow of sentimental tales, illustrations and articles in women's magazines, they would have recognised Mariana as the fair and noble embroideress of a glorious chivalric past, made familiar to them through the pages of *The Art of Needlework*, by Mrs Elisabeth Stone. This was the first history of embroidery, and it aroused great interest from the moment of its publication in 1840. Mariana might indeed have stepped straight out of the longest and most high-flown chapter in the book, 'Needlework of the Times of Romance and Chivalry', in which the author described the 'costly and delicate work' of 'courtly dames', and gallant knights 'adorned by the willing fingers of the fair'

with scarves fluttering from their helmets as they rode in 'pageants and triumphs, tournaments and games'.

Before embarking on a lyrical account of embroidered favours and tokens of love – compulsive reading for ladies whose willing fingers were busy stitching slippers, braces, smoking caps, cigar cases and watch tidies for husbands and fiancés, real and hoped for – Mrs Stone made her readers aware of the gulf that separated them from the needlewomen of those far off days. Quoting from a contemporary historian, she pictured the busy mistress of a medieval household engaged in the making and embroidering of dress and furnishings, and emphasised the contrast with 'the present day, when articles of every kind are obtainable in any country town'.

Opposite In Mariana, *Millais romanticised the medieval embroideress 'shut up in her lofty chamber', where, as the Revd C. Hartshorne wrote (in* English Medieval Embroidery, *1847), 'the needle alone supplied an unceasing source of amusement'*

Cigar case in appliqué from The Treasury of Needlework, *1855*

Man's waistcoat embroidered with flowers in tent stitch, c.1850

of furnishing fabrics into the shops, and by the 1830s machines which could imitate the effects of hand embroidery were producing dress materials at affordable prices. The rapid industrialisation of England, or, as Mrs Stone more poetically put it, 'Inventions rare, Steam towns and towers' and the prosperity it engendered had effected a revolution in the lives of her readers – many of them from the middle classes who had only recently moved up the social scale, and who had taken to embroidery as evidence of their genteel status and their husbands' affluence.

Needlework, like drawing and music, was highly recommended as an accomplishment for young ladies in the many etiquette books published to explain the niceties of genteel behaviour to the expanding middle classes. In *Domestic Duties* (1825), Mrs Fanny Parkes found such accomplishments invaluable for keeping a young wife 'innocently and cheerfully occupied', and useful too in 'whiling away the hours of solitude which would otherwise be spent in listlessness, indolence and discontent' when husbands were away from home. Firmly, she stated that 'the greater part of a woman's life ought to be and necessarily must be passed at home'. Home was the undisputed centre of Victorian life, and its decoration and furnishings – especially in the drawing room, where needlework proliferated on every surface and in every corner – were visible proof of prosperity. With more comfort than ever before, and with servants in even quite modest homes to release them from everyday tasks, Victorian women could identify with the grandest of Mrs Stone's embroideresses, as they too were 'removed from any necessity of its exercise'. Like the tragic but inspiring Mary, Queen of Scots, and like Matilda, 'the fond and affectionate wife glorifying her husband's glory' in the embroidery of the Bayeux Tapestry (now acknowledged to have been commissioned by Odo, William the Conqueror's half brother, and made, not by Matilda, but by professional embroiderers), they could indulge their fancy in needlework, thus displaying their newly acquired refinement of taste.

But the needlework that occupied their leisure hours had undergone a dramatic change since the last century – made plain in the catalogue of the textile section of the Great Exhibition which opened to the public in May 1851, the same year in which Millais' *Mariana* was shown at the Royal Academy. The Great Exhibition, presented in the Crystal Palace in Hyde Park, was visited by over six million people – their journeys made swift and easy by the spreading network of railways. For the many thousands of female visitors, the textile section must have been a principal highlight. Here was an unprecedented opportunity to admire the work of domestic embroiderers (mainly women, but some men), proudly displayed side by side with commercial pieces from the foremost firms, and a chance to compare the designs, materials and accessories offered by competing manufacturers both British and foreign. Despite the low standard of design,

The status and qualities of embroidery, and the attitudes of embroiderers had indeed evolved immensely in the course of the nineteenth century, affected by radical changes in British society. The advance of industrialisation and mechanisation – steam engines, railways, gas lighting, for example – affected embroidery through the invention of the sewing and embroidery machine. At the same time, the social effects of the change from a largely rural to a largely urban population, and the parallel growth of a prosperous middle class, eager to share in and emulate the activities and amusements of the upper class, gave needlework a special appeal.

The mechanisation of the textile industry which had begun at the turn of the century had brought a vast range

The Victorian embroiderer's fascination with romantic ideals of chivalry is shown in Alison De La Bere's watercolour of 1884 (left), *and a fourteen year old girl's Berlin woolwork picture of Mary Queen of Scots and her knights with the dying Douglas* (above). *Wools highlighted with silk and pearls, 1851*

few needlewomen can have left the Great Exhibition without some new project or purchase in mind, and the boost to sales was prodigious. There was now a mass market for needlework, and commercial interests therefore came to influence design to an extent not known before. In the 'Embroidery' section of the Exhibition there were examples of work in silk and metal thread, and on Houldsworth of Manchester's stand the 'latest specimens of patent machine embroideries, consisting of quilts, table-covers, curtains, panels, medallions, etc' could be examined. The first embroidery machine was the brainchild of Josué Heilmann of Mulhouse in 1828, but his invention was not put into operation until 1829 when he sold out to Messrs Koechlin, from whom Henry Houldsworth bought the exclusive rights in the same year, when the machine was patented in England.

The ominously named 'Industrial Work' section was devoted to 'Berlin woolwork, Needlework and Miscellaneous', and here the exhibitors demonstrated their taste for the romantic and sentimental in such scenes as *Bolton Abbey in Olden Time* after Landseer, and episodes from Sir Walter Scott's *The Talisman* and *The Abbot*, in particular *Mary, Queen of Scots Mourning over the Dying Douglas at the Battle of Langside*, which was

The girl mourning her pet goldfinch 'starved to death in a cage', after a pastel by John Russell, demonstrates Miss Linwood's 'matchless' skill at needlepainting. By 1908 Mrs Emily Lowes thought she deserved to be 'boiled in oil' for excessive realism

worked in four different versions. These pictures were meticulously rendered in Berlin woolwork, then at the height of a craze unparalleled in the history of embroidery.

The patterns for Berlin woolwork differed from any previously devised, in that they were gaily painted, or later printed, on squared paper, each square representing a cross or tent stitch. Unlike a design drawn out in outline on canvas, which would require the embroiderer to interpret it in colours and stitches of her own choice, the squared patterns needed only to be accurately counted to reproduce realistic effects similar to those so much admired in contemporary painting, or in the lifelike

needlepaintings of Miss Linwood, whose collection of nearly a hundred pieces had been one of the sights of London until her death in 1845. The ease of following Berlin patterns attracted many newcomers to embroidery, and was trumpeted by writers and manufacturers alike.

Many of the floral designs that appeared early in the century – the first, according to Mrs Stone, was produced by Philipson, a Berlin print-seller in 1804-5 – were not only colourful but extremely pretty; they looked attractive made up as cushions, small fire-screens, bags, braces and so on, and it is easy to see why the vogue caught on, especially when brilliant coloured 'Zephyr' yarns known in this country as 'Berlin' wools were specially imported from Germany for working the patterns.

Nowhere has the seductive appeal of Berlin woolwork for Victorian women been better explained than in Miss Lambert's *Handbook of Needlework* (1842), the first practical manual ever written for embroiderers. With long experience gained in the running of a London needlework business in New Burlington Street, Miss Lambert understood the pitfalls, as well as the pleasures, of Berlin work. She recommended the Zephyr wools for their 'fineness, softness and flexibility', but she sensibly pointed out that the harsher English worsteds made more hard-wearing backgrounds. While enthusing over the 'unequalled brilliancy and variety of shades' in which the wools were dyed, she also gave valuable practical advice on selecting colours, canvases and frames, and choosing needles with the right sized eye to avoid dragging the wool. In 1842, when her book appeared, the trickle of Berlin patterns

had turned into a flood, and the vast choice of materials and designs in specialist shops like Wilks' (established in 1832 at 186 Regent Street, in London, and the largest importer of Berlin work) must have seemed quite daunting to the novice. Miss Lambert calmly discussed the respective merits of silk, cotton, jute, woollen and Penelope or double canvas, all of which were available in different widths and sizes of mesh, and explained which designs would best enlarge or reduce.

Patterns and the materials for working them were generally selected in the specialist shops known as repositories, but when, in the 1860s, pull-out patterns began to appear as a sales ploy in periodicals such as *The Englishwoman's Magazine* (first published in 1852 by Samuel Beaton at the bargain price of twopence), shops which had agreed to supply the materials as a form of kit, or send them by post, were sometimes indicated on the design, making it possible for needlewomen living in the

Suggestions for Berlin and fancy work proliferated in Victorian women's magazines. The flower stand with fishbowl and fish-embroidered border (above), *a watch pocket with appliqué strawberries* (above right), *and a lid for an elaborate work-basket* (below right) *appeared in* The Young Englishwoman, *1874*

The brilliant colours of Berlin woolwork – as shown in this cushion cover, pattern, bags and samplers from the Embroiderers' Guild Collection – attracted many newcomers to embroidery. The samplers, (rolled up when not in use) were worked by both amateurs and professionals and reveal an unexpectedly inventive range of stitches and motifs. Note the imitations of tartan and lace

Opposite The Lion in Love *by Abraham Solomon (1858). Frames were 'permanent occupiers' in many Victorian boudoirs*

remotest country areas to join in the craze. Personal shoppers, confronted by the 'superb assortment' in big repositories like Wilks', must have found the professional samplers worked to show small sections of patterns in a variety of wools and on the many different types of canvas extremely helpful.

The finest mesh demanded sharp eyes, as well as determination and perseverance; anyone with less than perfect sight must have wondered, like Miss Matty in Mrs Gaskell's *Cranford*, 'if she could discover the number of shades in a worsted work pattern, or rightly appreciate the different shades required for Queen Adelaide's face'. In many Victorian interiors windows were elaborately draped with deep-fringed and tasselled valances and voluminous curtains; machine-sprigged muslin or net filtered the light, so that even in daytime, counting squares and matching wools to complicated patterns was problematical. The coy young lady in Abraham Solomon's painting *The Lion in Love* has placed her frame to catch the shaft of sunlight, and though it is not possible to make out the subject of her embroidery, the opulent furnishings of the room, and the gleaming mahogany frame suggest that she has chosen one of the most expensive and exclusive designs – prices covered an extraordinary range, from a few pence to around forty pounds. The cupid aiming an arrow at her elderly admirer perches on the

swirling gilt frame of a neo-rococo mirror between two
candles in typically over-ornamented holders.

Although gas lighting had been introduced into many
homes by 1858 when this picture was painted, it
produced a flickering and malodorous light, and even
when supplemented by colza oil lamps (introduced in
1834) many people still preferred candles for reading and
close work. In her *Life of Charlotte Brontë*, Mrs Gaskell
describes the Brontë sisters sewing by candlelight till nine
o'clock at night, after which candles were extinguished
for economy's sake, and the girls put away their work,
'their figures glancing into the firelight and out into the
shadow, perpetually'. By 1838 most candles were

Above left *A 'Musnud for a
Sofa' an 'Indian'-inspired
cushion in patchwork from
the* Treasury of
Needlework *(1855)*

Above *A colza oil lamp
lights the drawing room in
this photograph, c.1860,
showing an early sewing
machine*

machine made, with plaited cotton wicks which did not smoke or need snuffing. As late as 1877, Mrs Orrinsmith, author of *The Drawing Room, its Decoration and Furnishing,* was complaining about the expense of colza oil lamps and 'their inconvenient habit of getting out of order'. She found it difficult to understand why candles had given way to gas and oils when the former were less costly, cleaner and never needed repair. In Mrs Gaskell's novel *North and South* (1855), 'Candles had been brought and Fanny had taken up her interminable piece of worsted work over which she was yawning'.

Watercolour of Florence Nightingale and her sister Parthenope by William White, c.1836. Scrolling patterns were popular in Berlin woolwork

Mrs Gaskell's daughters, May and Meta, learned worsted work, and sewed in the evenings while their mother read aloud to them. Mrs Gaskell embroidered herself, and like many of her contemporaries, she did not differentiate between the terms worsted-work and Berlin woolwork. In August 1831, she wrote to Harriet Carr after a visit to Liverpool, 'I thought I would get some coloured cloth to

Fashion plate from La Mode, *September 1839, showing a lady working on a frame watched by a* *gentleman in a 'Persian' dressing gown and smoking cap*

Vibrant-hued flowers on an unmade-up chair-back worked in dazzling, aniline-dyed wools on a beaded ground, c.1860. *Discovered by William Perkin in 1856, these synthetically-dyed colours were much in demand, but faded disastrously*

work upon for stools, a la mode of some I saw the other day'. The stools she admired could have been worked with canvas tacked over plain material. In this variation of Berlin woolwork, the pattern was stitched through both canvas and ground, and when completed, the threads of canvas were carefully withdrawn so that the embroidery appeared to have been worked directly on the cloth. The contrast between the 'pearly' texture of the tent stitch and the plain dark ground could look most effective.

There is no-one in the Victorian period quite comparable to Mrs Delany in the eighteenth century to tell us about the minutiae of the embroiderers' world. Considering the huge numbers of women engaged in needlework of some kind, entries in diaries and letters are curiously infrequent, making novelists' contributions to our knowledge all the more valuable. The Brontë sisters, Trollope, George Eliot and Mrs Gaskell all throw light on the subject. Mrs Gaskell, for example, brings the obsessive Berlin enthusiast vividly to life in *Wives and Daughters* (1866), in the shape of the infuriating Mrs Gibson 'at her everlasting worsted work frame'. On rising to receive a caller, she upsets her basket of wools, and embarrasses her unwelcome visitor by insisting on picking up everything herself. She was given to counting stitches 'aloud and with great distinctness and vigour', and broke into conversations with 'remarks about the pattern of her worsted work'. Her behaviour evokes the maddening wife described by a husband driven wild by Berlin woolwork in a poem which appeared in M.T. Morrall's *History of Needlemaking* in 1852:

> The other day when I went home no dinner
> was for me
> I asked my wife the reason; she answered,
> 'One, two three',
> I told her I was hungry and stamped upon the
> floor
> She never even looked at me, but murmured
> 'One green more'.
>
> Of course she made me angry – but she didn't
> care for that,
> And chatters while I talk to her 'A white and then
> a black
> Seven greens and then a purple – just hold your
> tongue my dear
> You really do annoy me so, I've made a wrong
> stitch here'.

Equally vexing is the fact that her creations are all 'touch me not affairs' intended for display rather than use. 'The Wife's Answer' sets out to explain his mistake in thinking 'worsted work is all the ladies do'. She has plenty 'to do about the house', supervising the children, feeding the canary, practising 'that concerto thing', sending out dinner invitations, and only then sorting out her wool.

Lightheartedly, she justifies her hearth-rugs, cushions, bags, ottomans and innumerable chairs by repeating that all were done to please him, and ends her 'Answer', tongue in cheek, with the reassuring couplet,

> The loving wife, right cheerfully, obeys her
>   husband still,
> And will ever lay aside her frame to meet his
>   lordly will!

Whether loving or resentful, upper- and middle-class wives and daughters had little or no opportunity to do other than obey their husbands or fathers, as they were dependent on them financially. Until the Married Women's Property Act in 1882, husbands could dispose of their wives' property, inherited wealth and any earnings they might make. But the likelihood of earning was slight indeed when it was considered improper and injurious to the husband's social standing for wives and daughters to work. If financial disaster forced them to earn their living, almost the only acceptable option was to become a governess – and as a result this type of employment was hopelessly over-subscribed and shamefully underpaid.

Daughters had no choice but to stay at home until they married, and their parents' main objective was to ensure that they married well. 'They scheme, they plot, they dress to ensnare husbands', wrote Charlotte Brontë in *Shirley* (1849), and once 'ensnared', etiquette books and magazines were full of advice on 'How to Manage a Husband'. This was the title of an article in *The Ladies Companion* on 1 March 1851, warning young wives against neglecting the trifles 'which ensure the dependence of a husband' – for example, 'the fancied necessity of completing a leaf in

her tiresome Berlin work will sometimes be the cause of an uncomfortable and discontented evening. Most men have an absolute dislike of seeing work about'. Two decades later the warning was repeated almost word for word in a piece on 'Bored Husbands' in *The Ladies Treasury* (2 August 1869), recommending wives to finish their needlework during the day to avoid 'dull silent evenings' broken only by the infuriating 'click of the needle'.

By this time, the craze for Berlin woolwork was dwindling, but disapproval had been expressed by both men and women long before it petered out in the 1870s. 'It is simply copy, copy, stitch by stitch', wrote the Revd T. James in 1855 describing the increasing vulgarity of the Berlin patterns, 'Fancy work without the slightest opportunity to exercise the fancy. Dull task work unenlightened by one spark of freedom or grace'.

In February of the same year the first of three important articles 'On Design as applied to Ladies Work' in *The Art Journal* made a similar attack on the 'barbarous' copying of pictures, and 'the chaotic assemblage of gaudy and crude colours' in Berlin work. The author, Mrs Merrifield (whose book *Dress as a Fine Art* had appeared the previous year), regretted that fancy work was practised by ladies merely as 'the amusement of an idle hour', without any thought being given to its design. She made fun of the most flagrantly bad designs, and also – which was far more important – tried to explain *why* they were bad. She was convinced that if needlewomen had some knowledge of the rules of ornamental design, they would be able to differentiate between the good and the indifferent patterns on offer, and that 'some would invent their patterns if they knew how to set about it'.

Mrs Merrifield found the Indian apron (far left) *harmonious and well-designed, whereas spirals marred the flat patterning of the Turkish scarf* (left)*. The 'fox' slipper pattern* (below left) *was 'another instance of misapplied design... frequently exhibited in shop windows'. 'Is it usual for a fox to have two tails?' she enquired, and asked the reader to 'imagine the effect produced on a stranger by meeting unexpectedly a gentleman whose lower extremities were encased in these counterfeit foxes' heads'*

A Berlin travelling bag imitating a carpet pattern, and patterns for a table cover in braidwork from the Treasury of Needlework

Anticipating William Morris, she urged her readers to consider the fitness of the design for its intended purpose; she recommended flat, rather than three-dimensional, designs for flat surfaces, and pointed out the absurdity of choosing the standing figure of the Prince of Wales (the royal family and their pets were especially popular subjects) for use on a footstool, so that he appeared to be 'lying on his back and looking upwards'.

Well ahead of her time, she explained the importance of texture in needlework, but warned against imitating one material in another. Imitations of lace and tartan were popular in Berlin work at the time, and the tastelessness and poor design of many of the items illustrated in Mrs Warren's and Mrs Pullan's *Treasury of Needlework,* which appeared in the same year as Mrs Merrifield's articles (1855), make it clear how much Victorian embroiderers were in need of her guidance.

Determined to make her readers think before buying a pattern and stitching mechanically, she illustrated an Indian design, and explained in detail why it worked so well. She suggested they should look at the geometric

designs for tiles and bookbinding in back issues of *The Art Journal* as a source for their own patterns. Today, the idea of new uses for old patterns is commonplace, but in 1855 it was highly innovative, and must have provided welcome inspiration for anyone with a desire to experiment.

Almost without exception, the ladies who read Mrs Merrifield's articles would have made one or more samplers as children, and though many of the surviving examples are tediously repetitive exercises in spelling, counting and marking, worked entirely in cross stitch (now often referred to as sampler stitch), others reveal some feeling for colour and pattern, and are more individual in the choice of inscription and motifs.

The Brontë sisters each made two samplers during the 1820s, choosing biblical texts mainly from the *Book of Proverbs* and working them neatly in cross stitch on grey canvas, unadorned except for a geometrical border on Emily's and Anne's examples. They can still be seen at the Brontë Parsonage Museum, together with those of their mother and aunts. When their mother died in 1821, their Aunt Branwell came to look after them, and it was she who taught them to sew, and set them off on their samplers. The long hours passed in cross stitch stuck in Charlotte's memory. 'It would make a kitten dull to be mewed up so', says Sarah, the servant in *Shirley,* commiserating with the young Caroline Helstone who has been made to sit at her work all day.

However affectionate, Victorian parents often demanded absolute obedience from their children, and most sampler verses continue to extol docility and humility, and warn of the imminence of death and the fleeting nature of youth. Occasionally the inscriptions are refreshingly personal, even humourous, as in Jane Grey's sampler:

> The trees were green,
> The sun was hot,
> Sometimes I worked
> And sometimes not.
> Seven years my age
> My name Jane Grey
> And often much
> Too fond of play.

Green trees are a feature in Elizabeth Herbert's school sampler, and in three related samplers made by pupils at S. Westbrook's School in Wales early in Queen Victoria's reign. The balloon, basket and birds in a tree were among the motifs depicted in Berlin charts specially printed in small books or charts for children, but the girls at S. Westbrook's School were fortunate in having a teacher who appreciated more inventive stitchery, and encouraged her pupils by letting them choose biblical subjects or amusing vignettes (or both if they preferred, Margaret Morgan's sampler preserved at St Fagans near Cardiff

Nothing in my hand I bring
Simply to thy cross I cling,
Naked come to thee for dress:
Helpless look to thee for grace
Guilty to the fountain fly:
Wash me saviour or I die

Elizabeth Herbert Aged 11 Years
1838

Elizabeth Herbert's sampler, charmingly worked in coloured silks in tent, long and short, stem and satin stitches, was made at S. Westbrook's School in Wales under the guidance of a good teacher who encouraged her pupils in their choice of motifs, and then helped them in marking out and stitching the design

combines Old Testament scenes with a vignette of the school teacher scolding one of the pupils), and then drawing them out prettily within a floral border.

The standard of education for girls remained as low as in Farmer Bragwell's day. Showy accomplishments continued to attract and impress parents, and skill in needlework was one of the few qualifications a schoolmistress or governess in a private home could offer. To make up for their own lack of education and training, teachers relied heavily on question and answer manuals, stuffing

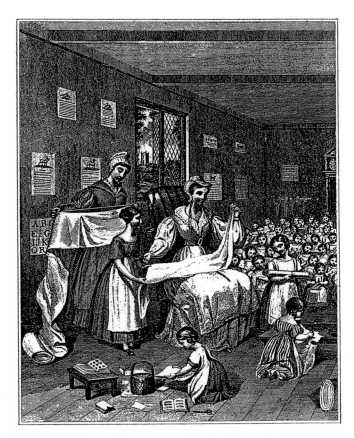

Left *Motifs drawn from Margaret Morgan's sampler, 1839*

A schoolroom in 1840 from The Workwoman's Guide

their charges' heads with snippets of unconnected information learned by rote. This sorry state of affairs was vividly summed up by Mary Grey, in *Thoughts on Self Culture* 1850, when she described schooling for girls as 'a tissue of frivolities . . . a patchwork begun without aim, fashioned without method, and flung aside when half finished as carelessly as it was begun'.

With stitchery on samplers reduced to cross stitch, patchwork was popular with schoolmistresses as it provided a useful introduction to seaming, hemming and running and instilled thriftiness in using up scraps of fabric. Patchwork was still a favourite pastime, appealing to all ages, and to men and women alike. 'I have made patchwork beyond calculation from seven years to eighty-five', wrote Miss Catherine Hutton, recording her needlework achievements shortly before her death at the age of ninety in 1845. Her last piece took nine months to complete and comprised '1,944 patches, half of which are figured or flowered satin, of all colours formed into stars; the other half is black satin and forms the groundwork'. Miss Hutton prided herself on making up her own patterns; and would have chosen the satins with care. Other enthusiasts liked to use up ill-assorted remnants for 'economical motives', without giving enough thought to the design. 'The industry of the worker is more apparent than her taste 'lamented Mrs Merrifield criticising their jarring efforts in *The Art Journal*. The needlework expert

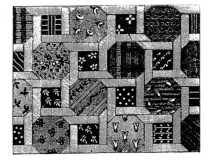

Above *Right angle,
Canadian, Puzzle, Twist,
Jewel and Mosaic patch-
work patterns from* The
Dictionary of Needlework

Below *Crazy patchwork
table cover pieced and
embroidered by Maria
Gordon Duff of Carnoustie,
Fife, in 1888*

in *The Ladies' Companion* of 2 August 1869 recommended using just two colours, since 'utilising odd pieces of silk and cambric renders the completed work very confusing to the eye, and gives an untidy appearance to a room'.

With their homes filled with competing patterns on carpets, upholstery and covers of every description, and their eyes attuned to the strident colours of Berlin woolwork, few readers heeded this advice, succumbing instead to the gamut of colour available in inexpensive offcuts of velvets, satins, brocades and silks. Unlike the printed cottons used in Regency patchwork, these seductive looking fabrics were uneven in weight, impossible to clean and tricky to seam together. Many of the silks were 'loaded' to make them stand out stiffly in the flounced skirts and inflated sleeves of fashionable dress, but this made them disastrously prone to disintegrate when used in patchwork. 'Velvet and satin form the handsomest kind of work', wrote Sophie Caulfield and Blanche Saward in their comprehensive *Dictionary of Needlework* published in 1882. Certainly when new the glowing colours and contrasting textures of glossy satins, refulgent velvets and shiny silks looked rich and showy, especially in log cabin

Crazy or Japanese patchwork and the stitches used to hide the over- and underlapping edges illustrated in Weldon's Practical Needlework *c.1885*

Above right *Bag delicately embellished with flowers in gauze, c.1835. The maker worked her initials in ribbons on the reverse*

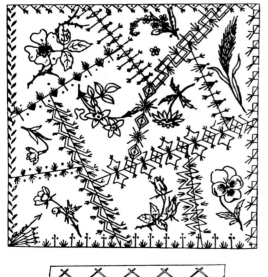

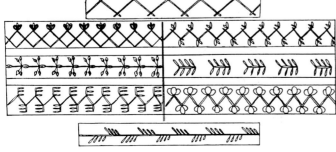

and box patterns whose three-dimensional effect was as intriguing to the eye as the realistically shaded and contoured birds and flowers standing out on Berlin work cushions and fire-screens.

In the 1880s the latest fad was crazy patchwork. Here the magpie instinct (which few embroiderers can resist) ran riot in the amassing of materials. Like Topsy in Harriet Elisabeth Stowe's *Uncle Tom's Cabin* (1852), quilts, bags, piano and table covers, even men's dressing gowns 'just growed'. There was no need to follow a design, as the pieces were arranged in as random a manner as possible on a firm but supple ground. Caulfield and Saward recommended ticking, a strong linen and cotton fabric, but old sheeting was often used. Variety and contrast of colour was the keynote, and the makers revelled in embroidering each patch with motifs incorporating glossy threads, and sometimes beads, sequins and ribbons as well.

The magpie instinct was cleverly fostered by the manufacturers of needlework materials. Embroidery had become big business; some manufacturers produced pattern books to promote their products, and a succession of novelties – shaded threads and ribbons, braids, beads, tools, fabrics and accessories – tempted the Victorian embroiderer whenever she set foot in a repository, or opened her favourite magazine.

Favourite materials included felt, which was sold in a pleasing range of colours ideal for appliqué, inlaid patchwork and small items of fancywork. Used imaginatively in combination with ribbon, chenille and aerophane (a delicately crimped silk gauze), it could create interesting textural effects, apparent in the garlands of wheat, flowers

A work-box becomes a 'garden' with scissors as 'statues', and a thread holder 'fountain' in Paddy Killer's drawing, inspired by the fanciful design of Victorian tools, including Tunbridge ware boxes, brass butterfly and bee needlecases by Avery and Son, tracing wheels and 'flower' pincushions in brass

Centre of a felt appliqué courtship quilt, c.1875-85

and leaves on bell pulls, sachets and dress ornaments; non-fraying and biddable, it was perfect for mosaic patchwork, and here the finest exponents were men.

In Victorian households, fathers and sons advised on geometrical layouts, helped in cutting templates and papers, and sometimes joined in the sewing. Three large specimens of mosaic work made by men were shown at the Great Exhibition, and their originality must have provided inspiration for others to try their hand. Surviving examples display scenes enlivened with an amazingly varied cast of real and imaginary characters. One of the most amusing depicts stages in courtship, from 'Hopes' to 'Matrimony', by way of 'Tiffs' and 'Jealousy'. It was given to the Victoria and Albert Museum in 1969, and, according to the donor, was made by a male relative to pass the time on a long sea voyage. The humour evokes *Punch* cartoons, and it is no surprise to find Mr Punch flanked by soldiers and an admiral in the border.

A significant novelty thought up by the manufacturers was the iron-on transfer, invented in 1875 by three employees of William Briggs of Manchester. This made it possible to transfer a design in a fraction of the time spent in pricking and pouncing or tracing. In the past, embroiderers had made use of whatever thin paper was available for tracing, but the invention of carbon paper 'in common use in shops for writing bills in duplicate' speeded up the process. 'The objection to it is that the colour may come off too easily', warned Elisabeth Glaister in *Art Needlework* in 1878. Miss Matty in *Cranford* (writen by Mrs Gaskell in 1851, but set in 1840) 'had been able to trace out the patterns very nicely for muslin embroidery by dint of placing a piece of silver paper [probably the kind used for cleaning knives with steel blades] over the design to be copied, and holding both against the window pane while she marked the scallop and eyelet holes'. These were typical broderie anglaise patterns, but in 1875 she could have transferred them by iron, as scalloped edgings were among the first transfers to be introduced by Briggs for children's dresses, underclothes and linen.

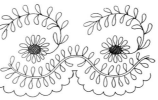

Whitework on a muslin 'canezou' featured in the Ladies Cabinet, *August 1834, and early broderie anglaise patterns from a manuscript book of 1820*

1851 Singer sewing machine on a wooden base

Despite the increasing choice of ready-to-wear garments, and the large numbers of dressmakers competing for custom, many Victorian embroiderers still derived satisfaction from working accessories and children's clothes, and many of their prettiest creations were in whitework. Though the exquisite Ayrshire embroidery, commercially worked on muslin with delicate and varied needlelace fillings, was beyond the competence of all but a few ladies, muslin with similar, if simpler, designs could be bought ready-traced in the needlework shops, and many other forms of whitework were explored.

The elegant fashion plates featured in periodicals like *The World of Fashion* illustrated ideas that could be adapted, and sales were boosted when paper dress patterns were included, some based on covetable French designs. The excitement of trying out the latest sewing machines 'by

*Bazaars provided
a market place for
fancy work. In James
Collinson's* The Empty
Purse *(1857), rose-
embroidered slippers
(left), matching braces
(right) and a Berlin
pattern are displayed.
The purse is beaded*

which needlework may be executed more regularly and with greater regularity than by hand' also encouraged the domestic embroiderer to embark on new projects.

Broderie anglaise was coarse in comparison to the Regency sewed muslins, but the formalised flower and leaf patterns looked fresh and attractive on crisp white linen or calico, and Richelieu embroidery was even bolder in effect. Both were derived from cutwork (see page 12), while 'Guipure d'Art' recalled the complex designs in renaissance pattern books. Special net could be bought for Guipure work, but netting by hand still appealed. 'My delight is netting purses', wrote Catherine Hutton to Miss Coltman on 1 November 1829. 'You will laugh at me, but the contrast of colours, and variety of patterns please me and interest me'. She netted over a hundred, a record perhaps, but purses were sold in large numbers at the charity bazaars that were a feature of Victorian social life

– especially popular with needlewomen as they provided regular opportunities to show off their embroidery skills and philanthropic interests at the same time.

Caulfield and Saward described netting and other techniques clearly, and in greater detail than in the popular magazines, and their *Dictionary of Needlework, an Encyclopedia of Artistic, Plain and Fancy Needlework* must have been a boon to experts and beginners alike. Entries ranged from advice on cleaning Berlin and crewelwork impregnated with the dust of countless coal fires (gin and soft soap, in the proportions of half a pound of soap to half a pint of gin' for the former, and tepid water in which a pennyworth of bran had been boiled for the latter) to information on historical and foreign embroidery, a subject of increasing interest at the time due to a remarkable revival of standards of stitchery and design in secular needlework.

This revival followed on from the transformation of ecclesiastical needlework begun in the 1840s by the Gothic revivalist architects A.W.N. Pugin and G.E. Street, whose designs were inspired by the great medieval embroideries. The secular revival owed its origin first and foremost to William Morris (1834-96), who abhorred everything about the cluttered, over-decorated Victorian interior and gaudy Berlin woolwork in particular. Morris determined to revive 'a sense of beauty in home life, and restore the dignity of art to ordinary household decoration'. He appreciated the way furnishings, especially needlework, could magically transform the interior, and

decided to teach himself to embroider. In the process he discovered a great deal about the potential and limitations of stitches and materials, and it was this practical experience, allied to his genius for making patterns that evoke, rather than copy, nature that enabled him to develop the unique style of embroidery we associate with his name.

Imbued with a deep love of medieval art and culture, he had admired the decorative hangings which were a feature in the interiors depicted in illuminated manuscripts, and he examined the intricate stitchery on old embroideries to see how such wonderfully rich textures were achieved. When, in 1859, he moved into his

St Catherine, worked in appliqué by Jane Morris as part of the scheme for Red House, but later mounted on velvet as a portière and lent to Burne-Jones for The Grange, his home in Fulham. The motif on her shoulder and elegant pose were inspired by study of the saints embroidered on medieval vestments

Morris & Co's showroom in Oxford Street, c.1879

Burne-Jones' sketch for hangings based on Chaucer's Legend of Good Women *commissioned by John Ruskin. They were to be made by Georgiana, helped by the pupils at a school run by Ruskin's friend, Miss Bell, but the project was abandoned*

first home, Red House at Bexleyheath, he wanted to evoke a similar effect, and was dismayed to find that shops could not supply the furnishings needed to create it. As a result, he lost no time in showing his wife Jane how to embroider, and together they set about making embroideries of their own, experimenting with stem, darning and irregularly worked long and short stitches in a daisy pattern on blue serge for the bedroom, and a series of panels depicting female historical figures for the drawing room. Experiments in silk and gold embroidery went on at the same time, and needlework came to occupy more and more of Jane's time. She clearly derived much pleasure from her own stitchery; on a boat trip on the Thames in 1880 she was, according to Morris, 'lying down and working quite at home'. Perhaps her most personal embroidery was the coverlet she worked in 1894, two years before Morris' death, for the four-poster bed at Kelmscott signing it with his motto 'Se je puis Jane Morris Kelmscott'. With curtains designed by their daughter May and valances inscribed with his own verse the bed is a moving testament to the family's love of embroidery.

Early in the 1860s Morris had also taught Georgiana, wife of his close friend, Edward Burne-Jones, 'what stitches and how to use them', and embroidery soon became part of life in the Morris circle. Georgiana worked him a jacket on his favourite indigo blue linen, and enthusiastically embarked on an ambitious narrative scheme inspired by the legend of King Arthur, designed by her husband for their London home. Gradually, what had started as an enjoyable domestic activity, with family and friends joining in, became one of the most admired and financially rewarding departments of Morris and Co, the decorating firm which made Morris' name a legend long before his death in 1896. The luxuriant furnishings displayed in the windows and showrooms of Morris and Co attracted the attention of rich patrons in search of exclusive schemes of interior decoration, and of needlewomen of different levels of competence, all eager to take part in the revival, now that embroidery was indisputably recognised as *ART*.

Morris emphasised the need to use 'especially beautiful materials' in order to create effects that were 'very rich and copius, or very delicate – or both'; the hangings, coverlets, portières and cushions available at the firm were worked in an exclusive range of glowing, specially dyed silks whose lustre enhanced the swirling effect of the stitchery, and made the Berlin wools that had once appeared so desirable look dowdy and unappealing. Affluent clients could purchase the expensive, large-scale furnishings with the embroidery completed in the workrooms, or commission designs to work themselves; but the prices for smaller items, such as cushions or firescreen panels, were extremely competitive (four shillings for a design traced on Manchester cloth in the 1890s), and embroidery enthusiasts of quite modest means could buy 'Morris' embroideries either with the design marked out on the material, or with a small section worked to show the stitchery.

Some of the patterns were intended for outline embroidery in stem stitch, which was simple in comparison to covering the entire ground with free-flowing darning and irregular long and short stitches, setting them, as Caulfield and Saward explained in the 'Crewelwork' entry in the *Dictionary*, 'so that each is put in with regard to its place in the whole design, and is neither worked too close to its neighbour nor too far from it, but by its own direction expresses the contour of a line, or the form of a leaf'. Few entries can have been perused more carefully, as crewelwork was the key to Art Needlework, which by the 1870s had become the latest craze.

'It is a great deal better in design than the Berlin work we used to do', says Miss Cherry in Mrs Oliphant's novel *Carita* (1877), explaining what was meant by Art Needlework, 'and it is a very easy stitch and goes quickly'. Most enthusiasts agreed about the improvements in design, but few needlewomen familiar only with tent and

Horned Poppy *screen panel worked by Mrs Battye in silks supplied by Morris and Co, c.1885. Through his experiments in dyeing, Morris achieved 'a marvellous play of colour' in his silks*

A four-panel screen illustrated in Mrs Glaister's Needlework, *1880*

cross stitch could have found the stitchery either quick or easy. To work a design as expressively as the *Horned Poppy* panel stitched by Mrs Battye (a regular and important customer at Morris and Co), demanded far greater skill than 'filling up little squares and diamonds ready traced in certain fixed colours on canvas specially prepared'. The phrase comes from Elisabeth Glaister's *Art Embroidery,* written in 1878 to encourage discriminating needlewomen to abandon ugly Berlin and fancy work, in favour of the 'greater refinement' of Art Needlework.

Persuasively written, and attractively illustrated in colour with bold, Morris-inspired patterns intended as 'hints and guides' for those with little experience in drawing and design, *Art Embroidery* was innovative and influential. Two years later Mrs Glaister followed up its success with further inspiring suggestions for furnishings in *Needlework,* which reached a wider public as it appeared in the popular Macmillan 'Art at Home' series. 'There will be a great gain to your house in originality if you arrange our own needlework for it', she wrote, urging her readers,

Designs for a curtain and footstool in crewelwork from Art Embroidery

120

A curtain from Needlework

in 1872 by a group of titled ladies with the dual aim of restoring 'the almost lost Art of embroidery to the high place it once held among the decorative arts', and at the same time of providing remunerative employment for needy gentlewomen. Inspired by Morris' example, the founders were determined to raise standards of design and technique. They commissioned designs from Morris and artists of the calibre of Burne-Jones and Walter Crane, and set up a training school where those who had been selected for employment were taught to stitch in the approved style.

If Berlin woolwork had appealed because it was easy and anyone could do it, Art Needlework caught the imagination because it required taste and skill and was therefore more exclusive. The aesthetically aware flocked to the School and its success was such that new premises in Exhibition Road were opened in 1875, and it rapidly became a centre of interest for domestic embroiderers. Here all the mysteries of Art Needlework were explained. In the Exhibition Room, visitors could study superb examples embroidered in the workrooms before deciding which designs they themselves might embark on. They could take lessons (a course of six in crewelwork cost £1.4s.0d) and buy samplers on linen containing various stitches which made practising at home far easier. The teachers brought along a selection of 'prepared and commenced work, such as cushions, chair-back covers, or footstools' which students could purchase and work under supervision – an ideal way to get started.

Marvellous displays of antique needlework were put on in the Exhibition Room, and owners of examples in need of repair could have them restored or commission copies. Lady Marion Alford, one of the founders of the School, was not only a fine needlewoman but an ardent historian and collector (her researches were published in

as 'thoughtful and cultivated people', to try some simple pattern making. Sensibly, she appreciated just how difficult it was for novices to devise and work original designs. If in doubt, she recommended they should go to the Decorative Needlework Society or the Royal School of Art Needlework at South Kensington where 'every care will be taken that your embroidery will be a work of art'.

The School was the most important and prestigious of a number of needlework organisations and societies founded in the second half of the century. It was initiated

Walter Crane's screen depicting the senses was worked in outline embroidery at the Royal School of Needlework (from Embroidery or the Craft of the Needle, *1899)*

Needlework as Art in 1886), and she insisted that the copies worked at the School should be exact reproductions rather than reinterpretations of the originals. 'Jacobean' hangings were a speciality, but though technically assured, they were sadly lacking in the spirit of seventeenth-century crewelwork. She travelled widely, and her scrapbook, full of drawings and observations on the needlework she saw, is preserved at Belton House in Lincolnshire, together with a handsome bed set ornamented with her initials, worked for her at the School, and a spectacular Japanese hanging embroidered with birds and plum blossom.

'At the present time few houses, I should think, can be without some specimens of oriental embroidery, whether Indian or Japanese', wrote Lucy, sister of Walter Crane, in 1882 in one of her lectures on *Art and the Formation of Taste*. She was commenting on the craze for all things Japanese in the 1870s and 1880s. Japanese needlework had suddenly become the height of fashion, and no one interested in embroidery could fail to have been excited by the thrilling examples displayed in the shop opened in 1875 in Regent Street by Arthur Lasenby Liberty, together with Indian shawls, Chinese robes and 'other marvellous lovelinesses of the East'. Folding screens in the Japanese manner became all the rage in 'artistic' drawing rooms, as contemporary cartoons in *Punch* make clear. Mrs Glaister

Opposite *Detail of a cover copied from an Elizabethan cushion for Lady Marion Alford by the Royal School of Art Needlework*

Above *James Cadenhead's portrait of his mother (1885) records the craze for Japonaiserie, both in embroidery and interior decoration*

George du Maurier's cartoon in Punch, *3 January 1880, mocks Japonaiserie in the aesthetic interior. Note the 'artistic' dress, sunflower tablecloth and screen*

A Japanese-inspired blackthorn design from Studies in Plant Form and Design *(1895)*

described a typical treatment in which 'each panel is a kind of suggestive picture. The more solid plants grow up from the ground, or out of very conventional water; higher up a bird flies across, or perches, and is balanced by a suggestion of cloud, a flight of distant birds, or a projecting spray or hanging branch of lighter flowers'. She suggested a satin ground worked with fine silk and gold twist, and she warned that 'care should be taken not to follow Japanese models so closely as to provoke a comparison with that inimitable handiwork, or to sink into servile imitation and so produce only a coarse copy of the original'.

'Coarse copies' featuring 'dank marsh rushes, wild ducks, storks and other objects of the same kind' (as a critic in *The Magazine of Art* described the increasingly hackneyed motifs in 1879) were soon flooding the market, as manufacturers and magazines vied for the attention of 'that large section of womankind which uses the needle for pleasure and beauty', and which had suddenly become aware that Art Needlework was 'much in fashion just now, and therefore they must by no means neglect it'. By the 1880s patterns demonstrating exactly the 'cheap and commonplace naturalism' that William Morris wanted to avoid were on sale in every department

store, together with 'artistic materials' rushed out to capture the market.

Antimacassars or chair-backs were especially popular, in drab rather than subtle colours. Lucy Crane deplored their 'barbarous coarseness; people seemed to have taken down the crash roller towel from behind the kitchen door, and made sprawling lines and blots or dark colour upon it, and then laid it out in the drawing room for the general admiration'.

Her comment is brought humourously to life in a passage entitled 'Worsted Work and Walter Crane' in the artist W. Forbes Robertson's autobiography *Time Was* (1931). As a boy in the 1880s he had a new governess, and with her came 'culture'. She encouraged him to pursue 'art', and he would watch her embroidering love-in-a-mist on antimacassars' – 'Love-in-a-mist is really bright blue, but in Art it was a grey' – and together they would visit the house of an old lady who was to be found,

> seated in a vast chair and surrounded by the implements of her craft, while about her, over the backs of chairs, round the edges of tables, pendant from the mantelpiece, prone on the piano, was on view her gallery of many and marvellous works.
>
> At her touch the furniture grew speechful and exchanged shy badinage. 'Where are you going to my pretty maid?' jocularly enquired the arm-chair, while the sofa coyly replied 'I'm going a milking, sir she said'; and the milkmaid on the sofa shot soft glances from her crooked woolly eyes at the bowing green coated gentleman on the chair.

We can get an idea of what this 'Wonderworker's' creations looked like from Walter Crane's *Spring* panel worked at the School, an intriguing late-Victorian version of the ever-popular pastoral theme.

Such obsessive industry was becoming rarer as the

Chair-back design from Art, Its Formation and Taste *by Lucy Crane, 1882*

Walter Crane renews the pastoral theme in Spring, *a screen panel worked at the Royal School of Art Needlework*

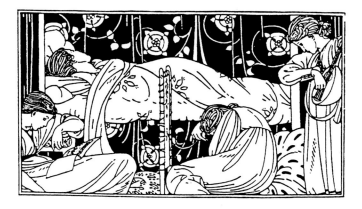

Above The Sleeping Beauty, *a prize winner in a competition to illustrate a fairytale in* The Studio, 1896. *The magazine reproduced many embroideries on romantic themes*

century drew to its close. 'It is not that artistic power has left the world but that a more rapid life has developed itself in it, leaving no time for deliberate dainty decoration or labours of love', wrote Mrs Orrinsmith in 1877. Dreams of independence, and of life with interesting pursuits outside the confines of the home, were gradually becoming a reality. For the 'New Woman' there were challenging prospects of higher education, going to university, travelling, indulging in sport and finding a job. The days when 'long hours had to be filled up' were over. As the leader writer in the *Daily News* put it in 1881, 'Modern ladies have a great deal too much to do with their time as to undertake such tasks as the Bayeux Tapestry for instance. Pens are much more in their hands now-a-days than pins and needles'. This did not mean that the 'passion for ornamental needlework' had come to an end, but that time had to be set aside for it. For the enthusiast, this made it more rather than less worthwhile.

The closing years of Queen Victoria's reign were full of interest for discerning domestic embroiderers. Few things stimulate the desire to experiment so much as seeing new and imaginative work, and with the founding of the Arts and Crafts Exhibition Society in 1888 there were regular opportunities to admire embroideries made by some of the most innovative designers and artist craftsmen and women of the day. Reacting against the mass production of the machine age, the Society's founders continued the pioneering work of Morris in making the public aware of good design and fine craftsmanship in beautiful things made for everyday use in the home. Needlework was a

The Victory, *the last of a series of four panels forming an allegory of the progress of a soul', worked by the versatile designer/craftswoman Phoebe Traquair, 1893-1902. The gloriously rich texture of laid and couched work and long and short, stem and split stitches in gold and coloured silks thrilled visitors to the Arts and Crafts Exhibition Society in 1903. The panels adorned her home near Edinburgh for thirty years*

Binding for Flora's Head *embroidered by Mrs Walter Crane, from an article on book covers in the first volume of* The Studio, *1893*

Entries for two competitions to design a cushion in The Studio, *1893 and 1896. Peacocks were especially popular motifs at the time*

feature of the exhibitions organised by the Society in London, and individuals, societies and firms were encouraged to show their latest work. The most striking examples were discussed in magazines such as *The Hobby Horse, Arts and Crafts* and, of the greatest importance, in *The Studio* which first appeared in 1893. *The Studio* promoted interest in embroidery by illustrating the work of amateurs and professionals, and holding Prize Competitions which anyone could enter with the chance of having their entry reproduced and commented on.

One of the most regular and respected exhibitors was May Morris, who had managed the embroidery workroom of her father's firm since 1885. A gifted designer and teacher, she played an important role in raising the status of embroidery. But she never lost sight of the quiet pleasures of domestic embroidery which she had enjoyed since childhood. Drawing inspiration from the coiling stems of the Elizabethans and from early Georgian dress embroideries she made charmingly decorated clothes for herself, table cloths and bed covers, and gifts for friends. Writing on 'Line Embroidery' (in *The Art Worker's Quarterly* of October 1902) she praised the delightful household embroideries of Italy, so different from those made in England 'for drawing room use and display', and

she concluded with a revealing personal anecdote. She had spent a night in a small inn in France which was dingy but run by amiable hosts. 'What pleased me most was to note my table napkin at dinner – of a coarse homespun linen. It had a hole or two in it, and these had been repaired by no dull darning, but by an exquisite little patterned lace stitch, frankly decorating while it filled the hole. It was a lesson to me both as a housewife and an embroideress'. It was this love of stitchery, together with a real understanding of a beginner's needs that makes her book *Decorative Needlework* (1893) so pleasurable as well as instructive to read. Explaining how to follow the curves and forms of a design in darning stitch she wrote 'the beginner will encounter several difficulties from the outset, and much more can be learnt by a few hours of personal instruction than by many pages of careful description'. Fortunate indeed were those who noticed her advertisement in *The Hobby Horse* (in 1880) offering private lessons in embroidery and were taught by her.

For needlewomen more interested in dress than furnishing embroidery, there were many ideas to be gleaned at the Costume Department opened at Liberty's in 1884. The gowns were softly flowing, in contrast to the tightly corseted line of high fashion, and made distinctive by the

Above *Christening mittens designed by Charles Ricketts and embroidered by May Morris for Daniel Sturge Moore, c.1900*

Smocked dress from The Children's Frock Party, *a Liberty catalogue of 1906*

discreet but stylish embroidery at the neck, sleeves or hem. Derived from historical models ('Medieval' and 'Greek' were especially popular), these artistic dresses could be purchased in the beautiful exclusive silks, cashmeres and velvets on sale in the store, but the style and embroidery were quite simple, and ladies inspired by the ideals of the Arts and Crafts Movement, who were also well versed in Art Needlework, could create their own versions without too much difficulty.

Some of the most attractive Liberty designs involved smocking which became popular for adults', girls' and even occasionally boys' dress in the 1880s and 1890s.

Smocking was one of the 'peasant industries' revived during the Arts and Crafts Movement, but in artistic circles 'delicate Liberty silks' were more likely to be smocked than tough linens. The words are Mrs Oscar Wilde's describing (in an article in the *Woman's World* in 1880) how the forgotten craft was rediscovered among the 'conservative rustics' of Sussex and Dorset. Weldon's hastened to bring out pattern and instruction booklets, and soon transfers with dots and cardboard gauges for marking the gathers were available for the domestic embroiderer.

Making and ornamenting one's own clothes ensured originality, and one of the best-known customers for Liberty's 'lovely stuffs' was Jessie Newbery, a most innovative designer and embroiderer whose teaching at the Glasgow School of Art was to transform both instruction in needlework and the entire look of embroidery early in the twentieth century. Like the Morris's with their furnishings, Mrs Newbery made clothes 'because she couldn't get what she wanted', and we may imagine that her experiments with appliqué on her own 'exceptional, unconventional' dresses, collars and belts helped her in evolving her highly distinctive style. She was the wife of Francis Newbery, the Principal of the Glasgow School of Art, and it was there in 1894 that she began offering embroidery classes to full-time students, teachers and 'happy women with two servants in the kitchen and nothing to do'. Her approach was radically different from the Royal School's, as she encouraged individuality in design. This was to become, and remains, an important subject for teachers and domestic embroiderers in the twentieth century.

The Twentieth-century Embroiderer

Embroidery is a very personal art, its charm lies in the individuality expressed by the worker.

Embroidery or the Craft of the Needle,
W.G. Paulson Townsend, 1899

Opinions on embroidery differed wildly at the turn of the century – the fact that so many were expressed being proof of the considerable interest in the subject at the time. Was it still thought of as an 'idle accomplishment' for

women to kill time as Lewis F. Day suggested in the preface to *Art in Needlework* on 1 January 1900? He went on to say that it was 'more than that. At the very least it is a handicraft: at the best it is an art'. Mrs Emily Lowes, writing in 1908, stated that 'needlework as a national art is as dead as the proverbial doornail', whereas Walter Crane maintained that 'in that remarkable revival of the arts and handicrafts of design', the craft of the needle, 'that most domestic, delicate and charming of them all, holds a very

distinct position'. This view was expressed in the preface to *Embroidery or the Craft of the Needle* (1899) by W. G. Paulson Townsend, but the author modified it in his introduction by saying that the art of embroidery, though still alive, 'has beaten a retreat . . . Today it is treated more as a graceful diversion'. He did however believe that it was 'a very personal art', offering 'endless scope and freedom for the imagination'.

The sheer variety, let alone the quantity of embroidery surviving from the period, shows that it could be all of these things. Domestic embroiderers of every age and class were engaged in projects ranging from the most ambitious pictorial hangings to items of fancy work suggested in magazines and in the flood of booklets brought out by commercial firms. Compared to their predecessors, they were spoiled for choice in terms of materials, patterns and tools. 'Art Needlework' shops and departments in stores flourished all over Britain, the name being proof of the continuing popularity of Morris type designs. The Royal School of Art Needlework had outposts in Glasgow and several other cities, and enthusiasts could choose between the many societies and organisations (thirty were listed in Dorinda's *Needlework for Ladies* in 1884) offering design services and classes, or acting as depots for the sale of work of embroiderers 'in distressed circumstances', on payment of a small subscription.

Opposite *Sidney Meteyard's* I am Half-Sick of Shadows *(1913) depicts Tennyson's Lady of Shalott, posed by his wife, graceful in a Liberty style gown, embroidering Sir Lancelot 'between the barley sheaves . . . as he rode down to Camelot'*

Above *The romantic image of the knight reappears in Mary, Lady Trevelyan's magnificent crewelwork panel, designed by John E. Pratt, and made for Wallington, which became her home in 1928. She depicts her legendary ancestor Sir Trevelyan, winning a wager to swim his charger to the mainland from St Michael's Mount. Like Lady Calverley's screen it is full of personal allusions. The shields bring together the families connected with Wallington, while many intimate details, such as her children's birth dates, were added as work progressed. Fortunately she left a key which visitors may read. Begun in 1910, the panel was completed in 1933*

129

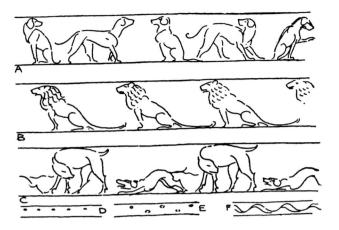

C.F.A. Voysey drew this formalised bird to illustrate an article on 'Conventional versus *Realistic Design' in* Embroidery *(March, 1934)*

Above *Ralph Hatton's simple drawing in* Design *(1902) shows how to suggest movement. Contemporary* *drawing and design manuals were full of hints for embroiderers – as valid today as at the time*

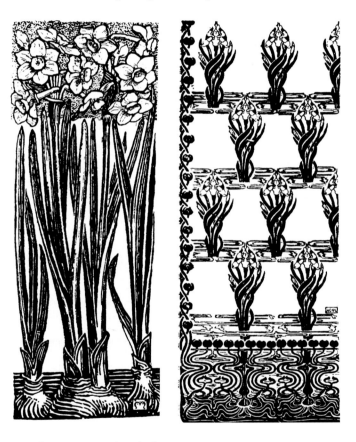

Ann Macbeth liked to use simple materials for household articles. This tea cosy (illustrated in Modern Embroidery*) was worked in knitting yarns on linen with a distinctive border in Chinese stitch*

Right *Jonquil and iris from W. Midgley's* Studies in Plant Form and Design

Sarah Grand's novel *The Beth Book* (1898) shows how helpful this could be in providing a measure of financial independence for expert needlewomen in difficult circumstances. Having 'thought out a piece of work, something more original and effective than the things usually sold in the fancy-work shops', her heroine spends her last coins on materials and starts work, discovering 'a new object in life' and 'a recreation that was more absorbing than anything she had ever tried before'. She has no money left for the subscription, but boldly sends off her work, asking that it may be paid from the sale of her embroidery. Fortunately her 'artistically beautiful design' seems 'sure to be snapped up', and the committee agree

to make an exception in her case.

'Artistically beautiful designs' continued to appear in magazines such as *Arts and Crafts* and *The Studio,* and many of the foremost artists and designers of the day, including Walter Crane, C.F.A. Voysey, Lewis F. Day and M.H. Baillie Scott designed for embroidery. Kits with 'artistic' designs printed on good material with the necessary silks and needles could be bought from Morris and Co, Liberty's and specialist shops like Pearsalls. As well as stocking oriental and near-Eastern embroideries and putting on stimulating exhibitions, Liberty's commissioned work from Ann Macbeth, an exceptionally talented designer who had been taught by Mrs Newbery. When

Mrs Newbery retired in 1908, Ann Macbeth took over the teaching at the Glasgow School. Much influenced by the School's distinctive style, her embroideries proved so successful that her designs were adapted as transfers, which were illustrated in the firm's catalogue and sold by mail order.

Patterns and suggestions for needlework in the embroidery columns of popular women's magazines show that fancy work was by no means dead, and the commercial patterns stocked by the less discriminating shops were often trite and repetitive. Grace Christie, who became the first tutor of embroidery at the Royal College of Art in 1909, was doubtless thinking of these when she wrote in *Embroidery and Tapestry Weaving* (1906), 'Nowadays much embroidery is done with the evident intention of putting into it the minimum expenditure of both thought and labour, and such work furnishes but a poor ideal to fire the novice'. Her ideal, and that of the most influential teachers, designers and writers on embroidery, was that amateurs as well as full-time students should, like the heroine of *The Beth Book,* devise their own designs.

The great stumbling block, then as now, was to be able to draw, and embroidery experts and writers of design manuals all addressed themselves to the problem of getting the beginner started. Grace Christie made design seem less frightening by explaining how 'All patterns are built up on some fundamental plan, of which the number is relatively small. The ability to choose, plan and arrange is in a greater or lesser degree inherent in everyone'. She assured her readers that for simple work, only a slight acquaintance with drawing was required, and that one of the best ways to acquire it was to make careful drawings from nature. The latter was also advocated by W.G. Paulson Townsend in *Embroidery or the Craft of the Needle* and Lewis F. Day in *Art in Needlework*. All three agreed that it was vital to study the past, but that blind copying of historical models was valueless. They were also unanimous in discouraging excessive naturalism and explaining the importance of stitches. Their views have been reiterated in successive embroidery books throughout this century, but seldom better or more lucidly expressed.

Stitches, as Mrs Christie so eloquently put it, were 'the language of the art', 'the means by which ideas can be expressed in intelligible form, and memories of all kinds of things be pictured on stuffs'. Their infinite variety and potential as a starting point for design had been brought

Below *Interesting stitches inspired Grace Christie's design for* The Meadow, *made for* Samplers and Stitches. *Animals in trellis, stem and French knots;* *hillocks in open button-hole; border in chequered chain band and raised chain band. The decorations* (left and right) *are also from* Samplers and Stitches

home to her at the wonderful exhibition of samplers put on by Marcus Huish in 1900 at the Fine Art Society in Bond Street. The exciting range of stitches revealed in two centuries of sampler making (starting in 1640) was a revelation to embroiderers accustomed to Art Needlework. The intricately looped, twisted and chained stitches of Stuart needlework were especially fascinating, and this exhibition was to inspire Mrs Christie in her writing, teaching and her own exquisite stitchery. She appreciated the way stitches could 'introduce new ideas for design' and urged her readers to take the stitches and 'see what can be done with them rather than to make a design with a pencil and brush and then see what stitches can be adapted to working it out'. Sampler making had been almost forgotten since the latter part of the nineteenth century, but Mrs Christie saw its value, not only for her students but for the many amateurs who used her books. The illustrations and working diagrams in *Embroidery and Tapestry Weaving* and her later masterpiece, *Samplers and Stitches* (1920), remain models of clarity, while those in Lewis F. Day's *Art in Needlework* are equally instructive and interesting.

Day was a successful and prolific designer and an experienced teacher. He was a founder member of the Arts and Crafts Exhibition Society, well versed in the theory of pattern making and ornament, but equally at home with the practicalities of the craft. He encouraged the domestic embroiderer to 'study old work to see what has been done, and then do it in one's own way'. Knowledge of design was essential, but he was concerned about the mounting pressure on amateurs to create their own

designs, stating baldly: 'You can only make all the world to be designers by reducing design to what all the world can do', and again 'To assume, then, that every needlewoman is, or ever can be, competent to design what she embroiders, is to take very small account of design'. *Some* embroiderers *would* develop a talent for design, while any cultivated woman could 'invent something better worth working than is to be bought ready to work', but others would find more satisfaction working with a designer. Both his wife and daughter enjoyed doing embroidery, and he was speaking from experience when he recommended the partnership of designer and embroiderer working fruitfully together, each understanding the other's needs. *Art in Needlework* reflects the family's love of 'reticent and unpretending stitchery, which, thinking to be no more than a labour of loving patience, is really a work of art'.

Needlework was very much a family affair in artistic circles at this time with husbands, wives, mothers and sisters discussing and collaborating on embroidery projects. The designer C.R. Ashbee and the artist Duncan Grant's patterns for furnishings were worked by their mothers, and Ernest Gimson made a number of designs for his family, including a charming sampler for his niece and a tea cosy ornamented with a rabbit emerging from its burrow. Experiments in their own homes fired the enthusiasm of important architects like Charles Rennie Mackintosh and M.H. Baillie Scott for embroidery on furnishings, and both men worked closely with their wives on refreshingly modern schemes. Margaret Mackintosh's distinctive lampshades, curtains and panels were the

Two treatments of the letter 'O' illustrating Lewis Day's ideas on 'Ornament as the Art of Everyday', and a sunflower curtain from Every-Day Art (1896)

Above left *Blackberry panel designed by W. Reynolds Stevens and worked by his wife, illustrated in* The Studio *(1903), one of many examples worked by members of the same family*

Above right *Firescreen in cross stitch designed by Duncan Grant for his mother to work. It was illustrated in* Modern Embroidery

Left *Appliqué furnishings feature in Baillie Scott's cottage bedroom in* The Studio *(1902)*

perfect complement to Rennie Mackintosh's revolutionary interior designs, while Mrs Scott's charming use of appliqué helped to create exactly the simple, uncluttered look her husband desired in his schemes. In 'Some Experiments in Embroidery' in *The Studio* (Vol 28, 1903), Baillie Scott wrote modestly as a beginner for beginners on 'the place of needlework in the house', providing decorating ideas that were well within the competence of the artistically minded. His closing suggestions for 'embroidery in the garden' in the shape of 'simple and broadly designed flags' to celebrate special occasions such as birthdays (each member of the family to have their own device) would surely have appealed to the inhabitants of Bedford Park, the first garden suburb.

There was further encouragement for beginners in another article in *The Studio* (1906) by Francis Newbery, Jessie Newbery's husband and the Principal of the Glasgow School of Art, celebrating the work of Ann Macbeth and at the same time extolling domestic needlework on ordinary household articles in everyday use which he feared were being supplanted by machine worked furnishings and linen from 'the art needlework emporium'. According to him, sampler making 'the heritage transmitted from mother to daughter' was becoming a thing of the past, and he regretted the loss of traditional skills. But in fact lack of teaching in childhood did not prevent adults discovering the delights of stitchery. 'I had had no formal training in embroidery', wrote

Peasant dress illustrated in Embroidery, *edited by Grace Christie in 1909*

Eve Simmonds' child's frock, embroidered in red on cream shantung reflects the contemporary interest *in peasant dress, both in its rectangular cut and decoration*

A baby's dress with sleeves and bodice in one piece, two bags and a sachet from Ann Macbeth's Educational Needlecraft

Eve Simmonds, maker of the exquisite little dress on this page. It was made for the baby, a boy, born to her sister-in-law Dorothy Peart in 1918. 'She also did needlework – everyone did in those days.'

In 1918 'everyone' included Queen Mary, who taught all her children canvaswork (the Duke of Windsor later referred to it as his 'secret vice'); children and teachers trying out Ann Macbeth's new method of imparting needlework skills (clearly explained in *Educational Needlecraft,* 1911), not by stitching samplers, but by making simple articles which gradually increased their confidence and developed their sense of colour; new-comers to needlework excited by the novel textiles displayed with idiosyncratically painted furniture on show in

Nymphs and Hounds Hunting a Hare *worked by Lady Ottoline Morrell after a design by Henry Lamb*

the Omega Workshops (opened in 1913 by Roger Fry who himself designed for embroidery); aristocratic enthusiasts such as Lady Ottoline Morrell, the celebrated Bloomsbury hostess, elegantly embroidering in the company of artists and writers at Garsington, and the Honourable Rachel Kay Shuttleworth, an expert needlewoman, busy teaching and assembling a fine collection of embroideries; and an increasing number of men, among them D.H. Lawrence, the actor Ernest Thesiger and Claude Flight, better known for his woodcuts and prints.

Lady Ottoline had embroidered from childhood; she had a marvellous, highly individual sense of colour and a passionate interest and feeling for textiles especially needlework, which she collected and re-used in the unconventional romantic-looking creations made for her by her maid Benty. Both Henry James and David Cecil commented on her 'Elizabethan' quality, and it is not difficult to imagine her in a flower- and obelisk-embroidered gown like the one on page 26. David Cecil described her as 'a creative artist of the private life, whose imagination expressed itself in the clothes she wore, the rooms she sat in, the social life that took place there, and more than anything in herself'. He does not mention her embroidery, but there is no doubt that this was a form of self expression for her, and the brilliance of the surviving examples is I think the most eloquent testament to her creativity. Henry Lamb made a number of patterns for her – she worked his *Deirdre of the Sorrows* while having treatment in Switzerland in 1912 – and a watercolour of tulips by

Duncan Grant was also probably intended as a design for her. Grant shared her enthusiasm for needlework, and sent her specially dyed silks and wools.

In early January 1913 her designs were being transferred to canvas by Mary Symonds, who was an authority on needlework and had a professional workroom in Oxford Street. She provided her with 'old bright silks' and gorgeously glossy floss silks in colours 'copied from an old Italian piece'. In a letter written a fortnight later, Mary Symonds promised to send more brilliant threads in colours 'like the Chinese', warning her that 'their first brightness goes off slightly'. These were used both for canvaswork pictures and a fire-screen, and for a marvellous coverlet in long and short stitch (as idiosyncratic as her inimitable handwriting), which she worked at Garsington during World War I, blending her 'interesting and vital ideas' in the gay silk flowers embroidered on it. Compulsive and generous, Lady Ottoline enjoyed making embroidered presents. She sent D. H. Lawrence a bedspread, and received from him a cushion cover embellished with a phoenix, and for Siegfried Sassoon she worked a picture of a young hunter designed by her friend Dorothy Brett. Once embarked on this project, she was so keen to finish it that she worked on through the night. As Juliette Baillot, her daughter Julian's governess, tells us, it 'had to be done by morning. I read the whole of Molière's *Tartuffe* into the small hours, while her fingers stitched the scene. It was wonderful'. Fortunately Sassoon found the needlework exquisite.

Marion Stoll's needlepainting of Lady Ottoline Morrell in a romantic moonlit setting demonstrates her belief that embroidery could express any mood. 'The idea is the thing', she told the reviewer from The Embroideress *when the panel was lent to an exhibition in Oxford in 1925, 'the stitch will come to order like an obedient servant'. Here she uses 'various forms of satin stitch' and an irregular split stitch*

Simply decorated housefrock by Lucy Revel illustrated in an article in The Embroideress *(1923) warning amateurs against weak floral designs*

With her enthusiasm for art and artists and her flair for needlework, Lady Ottoline would have been intrigued by the work of the avant-garde embroiderer Marian Stoll who captured her arresting presence in a stunning picture in 1924. Mrs Stoll visited Garsington Manor, the Morrell's home near Oxford, three times in 1923 and 1924, but sadly in her journal Lady Ottoline only records her early arrival on one occasion, rather than their conversation together. I feel that Lady Ottoline would have shared Mrs Stoll's belief that embroidery offers an 'inexhaustible field of new experience and joyous "adventure"'. It was Mrs Stoll's conviction that 'the only work which has value is that which shows creative inspiration. We all admit this in regard to every other form of art – it is really high time we admit it in regard to embroidery'. This was how she ended an article on 'Modern Design in Embroidery',

described as 'perhaps rather in the nature of a bombshell' by the editor of the excellent new magazine *The Embroideress* in which it appeared in 1928. Marian Stoll criticised the 'mortifyingly low' standard of English, as opposed to Continental, work and the dependence of Englishwomen on copying old designs, rather than producing embroidery 'representative of our own time'. She fully appreciated the difficulties of designing – 'very few embroideresses have sacrificed the years of stiff training necessary for good design – and advised the amateur to support one of the many good young designers in England, assuring her of the 'pleasure and profit she will find in the study and execution of his work. I say "him" and "his", as it is much better to get designs from a man who is usually ignorant of technique, for this will unwittingly set problems of execution that need intelligence

The ground of pulled fabric stitches was 'invented on the spur of the moment' in Marian Stoll's Dancer. *Mrs Lewis Day admired its originality writing on whitework in* Art in Needlework *(1926)*

and ingenuity to solve'. A bombshell indeed, provoking a flood of letters applauding or passionately disagreeing with Mrs Stoll's views. One reader defended needlework 'on Old lines', pointing out that in embroidery as in other things, '"There is nothing new under the sun" – and room for all'; another quoted Lewis Day's remark that 'perfect art results only when the designer knows quite what the worker can do with her materials', and asked the editor to reproduce one of Marion Stoll's original designs *with* her interpretation of it. Everyone wanted to see much more modern work, both English and Continental, and the first example reproduced in the magazine was a fire-screen designed by Wyndham Tryon and worked by Mary Hogarth.

Other well known artists who designed for embroidery included Paul Nash, and Duncan Grant, who worked with Vanessa Bell on the furnishings that contribute so much to the unique spirit of Charleston Farm House. Their daughter Angela Garnett recalls that they invented the designs 'merely' for pleasure and that they had the most elementary idea of embroidery stitches. Chance ideas would be noted down on scraps of paper, and then in the evening 'they would start doodling on a larger piece of paper, dreaming around the initial idea to produce one idea after another'. Duncan could work up one of these in colour in the course of a morning, but Vanessa worked more slowly, concentrating intensely on the simple shapes she had marked on tracing paper: 'It was fascinating to watch the trance-like gestures, and guess at the dreams that prompted them'. Ethel Grant, Duncan's mother, interpreted many of their designs, but others were rendered by Vanessa.

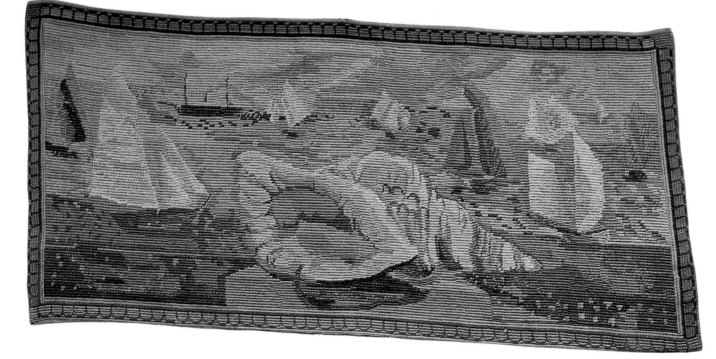

Panel designed and worked in wool with great subtlety of tone by Vanessa Bell, c.1935

137

Screen designed by
Wyndham Tyron and
stitched by Mary Hogarth,
expressing 'in abstract
forms . . . the music of
Bach and Wagner'. It was
reproduced in The
Embroideress (1929) after
repeated requests for
examples showing 'what
the needlework of today is
really like'

*Screen designed by
Wyndham Tyron and
stitched by Mary Hogarth,
expressing 'in abstract
forms . . . the music of
Bach and Wagner'. It was
reproduced in* The
Embroideress *(1929) after
repeated requests for
examples showing 'what
the needlework of today is
really like'*

D.H. Lawrence and his wife Frieda were another couple who enjoyed embroidery and who, according to Juliette Huxley (née Baillot), 'were adept at it'. In her autobiography *The Leaves of the Tulip Tree* (1986), she records happy hours 'in gentle creativity' when she and her mother were staying with them at a chalet at Les Arolles in 1915. Keen to join in this tea-time activity she managed to buy 'a sort of dishcloth which served as a canvas and some mending wools in various colours. Touched by the subtle but definite influence of Lawrence, I wanted to embroider Adam and Eve in their paradise; stitch by stitch the Man and the Woman stood by the brook, with the enchanted beasties around them and blossoming trees above pierced by God's gigantic eye. Lawrence finished Adam's genital organs which I had fumbled, adding a black virile business to a perfectly sensible phallus. He obviously enjoyed this last touch and the collaboration which crystallised these precious moments'.

That men should stitch for pleasure, rather than for profit (as the professionals had done for centuries), was a relatively new idea. 'Why is there this strange prejudice against men doing needlework?' asked Roger Grierson who was designing and working embroideries in the thirties, 'a man can do the design without loss to his dignity, but apparently the design must be left to a woman to do'. It was not always so. In Sarah Grand's novel *The Beth Book* (1898), Beth's Uncle James divided his day between occupations such as pigeon shooting and

recreation. 'For recreation he sometimes did a little knitting or a piece of Berlin woolwork, because, he said a gentleman should learn to do everything so as not to be at a loss if he were ever shipwrecked on a desert island.' This practical approach may explain why men took to netting and patchwork in the previous century. Though Dr Johnson was, in Mrs Thrale's words, 'a strenuous approver of embroidery', he teased both sexes on their attitude to stitchery, as she recalls in her *Anecdotes of Doctor Johnson* (1786). He held 'that one of the great felicities of female life was the general consent of the world, that they might amuse themselves with petty occupations, which contributed to the lengthening their lives, and preserving their minds in a state of sanity. "A man cannot hem a pocket handkerchief" (said a lady of quality to him one day), and so he runs mad, and torments his family and friends'.

During my research for this book, many men have told me how needlework preserved their minds in a state of sanity during two world wars, and how once hooked they never gave up doing it. The therapeutic quality of

Below left *In* Mary
Thomas's Dictionary of
Stitches *(1934) witty
drawings accompany the
stitch diagrams. Here
gentlemen at a dinner
represent hem stitch*

Below *Interesting
asymmetric stool design by
Anthony Betts illustrated in*
Modern Embroidery, *which
included a dozen designs
by men*

Tony Murray's Craigmore Orangery Garden *was inspired by the eighteenth-century Stoke Edith hanging at Montacute in Somerset. He substituted his* own house in nearby Somerton for the orangery in the original, and included his dog and a 'gardener' drawn from Rex Whistler's self-portrait at Plas Newydd. He took up canvaswork in 1962 when his wife handed over a piece she found 'too taxing for her eyes', and has not stopped since

139

stitching is well known by all who have tried it, and it was particularly valued by Ernest Thesiger who was already an experienced embroiderer when he was wounded during World War I. He determined to find employment for severely disabled and shell-shocked soldiers through embroidery, and this he succeeded in doing despite being snubbed by the Ministry of Pensions – who first expressed interest, and then decided needlework was 'an effeminate occupation'. In his amusing autobiography, *Practically True* (1927), he describes a female reaction to male needlework that would surely have appealed to Dr Johnson. On train journeys in France with a painter friend and amateur of 'petit point' and 'gros point', both men would enjoy working in an empty carriage. One day they were joined by a heavily veiled widow, who was so immersed in her grief that they 'bravely continued to sew'. The widow's sobs gradually subsided, 'Her handkerchief had been removed from her eyes and crammed into her mouth. The sight of two grown men deep in embroidery had overcome her grief. She was in fits of laughter'.

Thesiger was making a christening veil for his niece on this occasion, and his enthusiasm for needlework of all kinds eventually led him to write *Adventures in Embroidery* (1941), a treasury of ideas for furnishing, some inspired by old stitchery, others suggested by woodcuts, paintings, photographs, mosaics and theatre and ballet designs. 'It requires as much ingenuity to adapt

a design as to invent one', he wrote, 'and the needleworker who can adapt a pattern from another source is half way along the road to being a successful designer'. Firm in his belief that 'needlework is an outlet for the creative instinct', his choice of striking images still fires the imagination, and must have persuaded many wartime readers that they could indeed create rather than copy designs.

To be 'creative' and 'modern' was increasingly important, and no one seriously interested in embroidery could ignore the changes in contemporary design. The new look of embroidery was revealed to the public in an important exhibition at the Victoria and Albert Museum in 1932. Here was an opportunity to compare British, American and Continental work, and to watch well known embroiderers demonstrating popular methods such as appliqué, quilting and embroidery on net, and hear them talking about design. Among the highlights were three sessions on design and colour given by Rebecca Crompton, a compellingly original embroiderer and teacher whose strikingly modern panel, *The Creation of Flowers,* caused a stir at the exhibition, and was reproduced a year later in *Modern Embroidery*. This was a special number of *The Studio* prepared by Mary Hogarth in 1933 as a lasting record of the show. More than any other illustration in the book, *The Creation of Flowers* sums up what Mary Hogarth had to say about embroidery

Opposite *Fascination with Elizabethan history and embroidery led Jack Robinson to take up blackwork, explore the intricate patterns and then devise his own, as in this book cushion, 1992*

Right *Ernest Thesiger reproduced Eric Ravilious'* Summer Landscape *in* Adventures in Embroidery *to show how wood engravings can provide a starting point for embroidery design. Examples from the 1930s are rich in suggestions of stitchery*

Below The Creation of Flowers *was an experiment in textures, tones and colours . . . built up spontaneously without previous drawing. Satin, piqué, wool and silver tissue were applied, and the contrast of texture was heightened by ribbons,*

braid and buttons. Mary Hogarth admired it as 'an example of inseparable design and technique'

Appreciating that not everyone could draw, The Embroideress *continued to include transfers such as this horned poppy and hellebore*

being 'the invention of today' and expressing 'this age'. 'The technique should govern the design', she stated, and stitches should be 'our slaves not our masters'. Embroiderers had to move with the times, 'speed necessitating a more rapid technique'. She advocated simple materials and methods like appliqué to meet the need for hurry and economy in modern life. Her assurance that 'a poor thought, but mine own is worth more than a copy' encouraged her readers into thinking that they *could* design provided that they began simply. 'The counsel of perfection is to build up the design by stages on the material, and that the worker and the designer be one and the same person.'

This free experimental approach was taken several stages further by Rebecca Crompton in her challenging book *Modern Design in Embroidery* (1936). This broke all the accepted rules, and delighted the modernists as much as it infuriated the traditionalists. In it she explained how the embroideress could become a creative artist, and how she could express personal thought and feeling in individual work. With only a limited knowledge of stitches and none at all of drawing she could start experimenting and 'thinking in terms of embroidery'. Aided by lively drawings and thought-provoking stitched examples (which were on no account to be copied!), she explained 'the value of spontaneous expression', helping the reader to develop a sense of pattern and line, and to distinguish between good and bad shapes. As individual in her

142

appearance as she was in her opinions – she tried out her colour theories in her own idiosyncratic dress – she encouraged adventurous and imaginative use of colour, and insisted that success lay in 'the close study of the combination of form, colour, tone and texture in their special relation to embroidery', a view that remains central to the teaching of needlework today.

Rebecca Crompton's book received a mixed reception when it was reviewed in *Embroidery*, the journal of the Embroiderers' Guild in March 1937. The author was undoubtedly a courageous pioneer with 'an immense gift for design', in the same tradition as Marian Stoll, but – and here was the rub – lacking her technical perfection. 'Her main interest is in design and colour: stitches and technique are secondary matters to her', and the reviewer felt bound to add 'that neither her stitches nor her technique are her strong point'. However, 'for those who are exploring the possibilities of fresh design' she agreed that the book was very valuable, and might 'give a lead and an immense amount of inspiration'.

That a dynamic new approach was needed was underlined in three articles appearing in the same issue of the magazine. E. M. Friend, the art master of the Downs School at Malvern wrote asking how artists and craftsmen could help embroiderers 'to get more fun out of the designs they are working'. He criticised the 'dull and lifeless patterns' on sale in the handicraft shops, the embroiderers' dislike of change and their suspicion of 'even the best modern designs'. He praised the teachers whose pupils were 'designing patterns which put to shame those we buy', and suggested to the Guild that they should encourage artists to send in designs, and to sell 'pattern units printed on transfer paper to be put together in different ways'. This the Guild was already doing, as the magazine's previous article had shown. Here were examples from 'their ever-increasing supply' of transfers, with all sorts of suggestions for treating the same design in a variety of methods and stitches.

The third piece in *Embroidery* was entitled 'Our Daughters are not Taught Embroidery', and expressed the Guild's concern that girls were no longer being encouraged to take any interest in the subject. In many schools sewing and embroidery had been crowded out of the curriculum as a result of 'the passionate belief of the last generation that boys and girls must have exactly the same sort of education'. The Guild (formerly the Society of Certificated Embroideresses, founded in 1906 and reformed as The Embroiderers' Guild in 1920) was committed to furthering the 'love and practice of embroidery', and to teaching, and they asked parents and schools for their opinions. The replies they received showed how strongly readers felt about the subject.

Friend's plea for embroidery designs to be fun was echoed in Rebecca Crompton's teaching, and some of her most light-hearted ideas were for machine embroidery. She considered the sewing machine 'a most useful tool for

Opposite top *'Design showing the use of broken colour', from* Modern Design in Embroidery *worked in wools on flecked tweed*

Opposite below *Illustration from* Modern Design in Embroidery *explaining the value of line, which gives rhythm, life and direction*

Right *The modern-looking screen illustrating E. M. Friend's article in* Embroidery *makes a striking contrast with the Guild's transfers reproduced in the same issue. These provided 'an accommodation for those less gifted with the pencil'. New treatments were suggested for traditional designs*

a modern embroiderer both from the constructional and decorative point of view'. At the 'Needlework through the Ages' exhibition in Haslemere in August 1938, she showed an example of 'fine machine stitchery in white and silver, very delicate and charming, and containing among other delightful tiny details, a most attractively drawn horse'. This extension of the 'needle-in-the-hand' to the 'needle-in-the-machine' drew from the reviewers in the winter issue of *Embroidery,* 1938, the comment that the exquisite design would have been better 'worked by hand . . . handwork can still hold its own against the machine, not only by its variety and surface charm but in *finish'.*

In fact, embroidery worked on an ordinary domestic machine *could* create astonishingly varied effects, as the remarkable examples made by the Singer Sewing Machine Company early in the century show. The Embroidery Department specialised in copying marine paintings, landscapes and portraits which were used to advertise the versatility of the domestic machine. Amateurs who had admired the skill of the Singer embroideresses could come to the department for lessons in this version of 'Art Embroidery'. There they were shown how to remove the presser foot, cover the feed, mount the material in a wooden hoop, and then move it under the machine needle. These were straight stitch treadle needle machines, but with practice it was possible to work zigzag stitch, and the Singer employees were adept at imitating even the most complex effects of cutwork and needlelace.

For most people, however, machine embroidery was still associated with commercial work and mechanical results, and fierce controversy raged over its use in 'creative' embroidery. That it gradually became acceptable, and then, little by little, exciting, was due in part to Rebecca Crompton, but mainly to Dorothy Benson, who had worked in the Education Department at Singer since 1916, and understood its potential for the domestic embroiderer, once it was 'loosened up'. Dorothy Benson records how at first the teachers 'walked out in protest' while she was demonstrating in Rebecca Crompton's lectures. Her book *Your Machine Embroidery* (1951) did much to reconcile them, and to encourage amateurs to try it out. Sensibly, she began by explaining that it did not compete with handwork, and adding 'nor does it encroach upon it in any way. Each has its own important part to play and the two often go hand in hand. Each is lovely in its own way, and each type of worker should be able to appreciate the art of the other'. Even the most die-hard traditionalists must have found some charm in the delicate tracery of flowers on christening robes and the

Above Rebecca Crompton's Bird *was machine embroidered by Dorothy Benson. Compare the loose treatment with Dorothy's bird and horse drawn to illustrate darning stitch in* Your Machine Embroidery

Machine-embroidered table centre by Winifred Reed, who trained at Singer with Dorothy Benson, c.1950

A tea cosy in machine darning and crazy stitch on organdie 'which shows the stitch up well', from Singer Machine Embroidery

Right *Constance Howard's designing skill is apparent in these wood engravings she made as a student in the 1930s*

spidery convolutions spiralling effortlessly round table mats or curtains in organdie or voile as embroiderers discovered for themselves the pleasure and freedom of swiftly following the machine embroidered line.

The instructions in Dorothy Benson's first book, *Singer Machine Embroidery* (1945) and *Your Machine Embroidery* were quite clear enough to enable amateurs to experiment at home, but more than any other technique, it was easier and quicker to learn the rudiments in a class, with a teacher on hand to help with the apparent unpredictability of the machine. 'Embroidery is now based upon organised teaching instead of upon a tradition handed down within the home; and employs as teachers those who may be considered specialists in their work', stated Elsie Eraut, charting the progress of twentieth-century needlework in *Embroidery* in 1934. More and more women were going to classes, and the teachers who instructed them were more highly qualified than ever before. Having discussed the way this encouraged originality and 'freedom of thought and expression', Elsie Eraut struck a note of warning, suggesting that some teachers were becoming *too* influential – a danger resulting all too easily in the 'lookalike' versions of distinctive styles that we recognise today. Many teachers had trained at art school, and some had come to embroidery through painting, engraving or book illustration, and had considerable talent for design. As well as teaching, they wrote books explaining their methods, exhibited their work and aired their views in magazines. Little by little they have been shaping the look of embroidery and gradually increasing awareness of good design, as perusal of Constance Howard's magisterial four-volume history, *Twentieth Century Embroidery in Great Britain* reveals.

Below *Dorothy Buckmaster's fire-screen design was drawn for Daisy Lloyd who began by stitching the brown caterpillar, named Sweetie Pie after the Lloyd dachshund because of its colouring, long body and short legs. Worked on a blue ground, the screen was completed in her eightieth year, in 1960*

Above *Screen panel c.1929 by Kathleen Harris, who conducted the first course* *for the Embroiderers' Guild in 1933. Felt appliqué and sequins on hessian*

The Embroiderers' Guild in Grosvenor Street provided a meeting place where members and teachers could join in the lively debate over technique versus design initiated in *Embroidery,* and discuss the magazine's thought-provoking articles on the future of embroidery. Despite the requests for 'more modern designs', the weekly classes were devoted to 'Lessons in the Stitches of Embroidery'. These were open to members and non-members, and members who were 'improving their skills by practical work' could study the Guild's growing collection, borrow designs and books from the library and the invaluable portfolios containing worked examples of a particular method or period. For 'younger people and those for whom the fascination of embroidery has only just begun to dawn', the Guild provided a 'beautiful series of transfer patterns' as well as short courses of instruction. For those most interested in perfecting their technique, the Royal School of Needlework in South Kensington continued to offer private lessons and classes, as well as providing a design service. Both the School and the Guild were London based, but the latter was beginning to open branches, and the Townswomen's Guild and Federation of Women's Institutes had established a network all over the country offering instruction in needlework.

As in the past, many enthusiasts continued to work on their own, uninfluenced by the conflicting advice in magazines and books, and unimpressed by the transfers and new lines put out by the manufacturers. Some like Judith Lear, niece of John Everett Millais and a skilled artist,

found their inspiration in close study of flowers and the countryside, and developed a pleasingly personal style of stitchery. Another artist, Beldy (Mabel Maughan Beldy, sister-in-law of Somerset Maugham) experimented with collage, creating atmospheric images with great subtlety of tone. Beldy had studied drawing with her father, but keen embroiderers with no special talent for drawing or desire to create their own designs could always employ a professional sympathetic to their needs. Among the most accomplished but little known designers was Dorothy Buckmaster, who drew out the patterns for the furnishings

Spring Flowers *worked in coloured silks by Judith Lear, 1934*

Beldy's Carmen Amaya, ballet, *one of a series of collages inspired by the drama and movement of the dance, was exhibited at the Leicester Gallery in* *1948. The ballerina Tamara Karsavina admired her 'impressionist' treatment; she was still stitching at the age of ninety-two*

worked by Daisy Lloyd and her son, Christopher Lloyd, for Great Dixter in East Sussex where they are still in use.

During and after World War II embroidery materials were poor in quality and in short supply. Far from restricting creativity, however, the necessity to 'make-do-and-mend' led embroiderers to experiment with whatever came to hand, resulting in some interesting work, notably appliqué and patchwork. Innovative suggestions for using hitherto unthought of materials were made by the designer/embroiderer Lilian Dring in a series of articles in the periodical *Art and Craft Education* published during the first months of the war. These were intended for teachers to pass on to their pupils, but they were equally inspiring for adults. Lilian Dring urged a return to the 'Thriftcraft' of previous generations inventively re-using

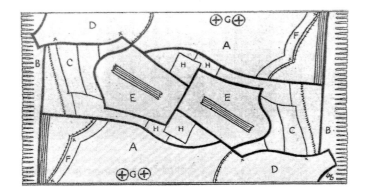

Lilian Dring's 'Thrift' rug (1934) was ingeniously contrived using the cut-out pieces of two old coats and *patches from other garments, with felt 'buttons' disguising the buttonholes*

both dress and furnishings, and she showed how with imagination, taste and ingenuity, the most unlikely fabrics – even blackout material – could produce not only useful, but beautiful results. These qualities were apparent also in her designs for the 'Patchwork of the Century' shown at the Women of the Century 1851-1951 Exhibition held in Twickenham in 1951. The one hundred squares recorded events, people and places of interest during the period, and were worked mainly by amateurs using only materials already in their possession – anything from tablecloths to service uniforms – nothing new was to be bought for the project.

The opportunity to work with a skilled designer in the company of like-minded enthusiasts is as challenging as it is enjoyable, and group embroideries, many of them recording the history and beauty of towns and villages, have become a feature of twentieth-century work. The New Forest Embroidery designed by Belinda Montagu and on show in the New Forest Museum in Lyndhurst is a particularly engaging example. The embroiderers who meet to discuss and work on the embroidery are continuing the tradition of realising ambitious furnishing projects within the household, as often happened in the sixteenth and eighteenth centuries. Work on the seven panels that make up the Bishops Stortford Mural began in the designer Leila Riddell's home, but rapidly outgrew the space available. By happy chance the designer and one of her most expert helpers, Bunty Abraham, agreed to exchange houses during the project, and the mural was completed and assembled in the spacious barn at Bunty's old and Leila's new home. One of the pleasures of such work is that it can incorporate all sorts of personal contributions, not just in the embroidery, but in providing information about local history, buildings and flora and fauna. The different species of trees were expertly drawn out by Jane Hall; like all the motifs they were worked on canvas and then applied as slips in the manner favoured by the Elizabethans.

It is interesting to see how other traditions and themes have been updated, and to note how familiar motifs, methods and materials reappear in a new guise in the latter part of the twentieth century. 'Each generation . . . must invent new forms to meet its outlook and needs', wrote Phyllis Platt in *Embroidery* (December, 1935). 'It is like mounting a spiral staircase and seeing the same view from different levels.' Take for example the pastoral theme, which has been so popular with embroiderers since the sixteenth century. In the sixties Kenneth Dow Barker was recording cows and sheep grazing peacefully in Cumbria entirely in darning stitch – a foretaste of the interest in landscape in the seventies. A panel of sheep nestling together created by Jenny Chippindale (see page 151) demonstrates the interest in texture and soft sculpture in the eighties, while Pod Clare's *Sheep in Bracken* reflects the continuing fascination with stitchery on painted grounds in the nineties.

The Bishops Stortford Mural *(made by 142 embroiderers, 1984-90) presents a panorama of the town's history from 1500 to the present. The central panel* (above) *depicts mid-Victorian houses and churches, worked in stitches chosen to emphasise the building materials. The distinctive statue of a white stag (emblematic of Hertford-shire) graces a building in North Street and the left-hand figure depicts Francis Rhodes. The mural hangs in the Rhodes Centre in Bishops Stortford*

In her crewelwork portrait of a house in the New Forest (1990), Janet Haigh reinterprets the rolling hillocks and multiflowering stems loved by generations of embroiderers. She follows a long tradition in recording the family's dogs and includes flowers from their garden. She suggests the Solent and Forest with boats, badgers and ponies

Right *Eugenie Alexander updates the story of* Europa and the Bull *(see page 29) using collage,* c.1958

Opposite top *Belinda Downes draws on the pastoral tradition in* Holme Pierrepoint Hall with Mermaids *(1991), where sheep graze in a field of applied flowers. Inspired by the 'wonderland' effects of Stuart raised work, she reinterprets the mermaids of the past in hand and machine embroidery*

Below *Kenneth Dow Barker's* Cattle at Kentmere *was worked in darning stitch in the 1960s*

Below Sheep in Bracken *(1992) was inspired by the countryside near Pod Clare's home on the west coast of Wales. The bracken stems were made by 'drawing' in dip-dyed* wool using a Japanese bunka bishu needle, and the fronds by applying lengths of a painted tassel yarn. The sheep is in loop stitches

Left *Sheep panel made as a City and Guilds project by Jenny Chippindale, 1980*

The fact that all these are pictures and panels rather than furnishings speaks also of changing aspirations, and marks a further swing of the pendulum from the useful to the decorative – as when picture-making replaced the vogue for furnishings in both the Stuart and late Georgian periods. But whereas the needlewomen of those days relied mainly on pattern drawers for their designs – which they then made individual by their choice of colours and stitches – more and more embroiderers in the closing decades of the twentieth century have risen to the challenge of creating their designs, as well as stitching them. 'It is a fallacy to think that original design can only be achieved after years of training', stated Constance Howard, conveying her enthusiasm in *Inspiration for Embroidery* (1966), 'With an open mind and unbiased thought a great deal may be attempted from the start.'

Many have found this to be so through joining a class and coming into contact with a gifted teacher; others have been inspired to attempt their own design through lectures, exhibitions, books, magazines and the occasional television programme. Once started, they have quickly discovered that embroidery is not 'just a unique method of decorating a textile . . . but is also a uniquely different way of expressing abstract ideas and aspirations shared by all decorative artists and designers'. The phrase is by Joan Edwards, concluding her *Chronicle of Embroidery 1900-1950* (1981), and pointing the way forward as she did in her remarkable ten-week courses at the Victorian and Albert Museum in the early seventies. These courses taught amateurs (myself included) not only a great deal about the methods of the craft, but also how to look at embroidery in the widest possible context, relating its design to the other decorative arts of succeeding periods, and in the process providing endless possibilities for personal projects and research.

Today's embroiderers are offered an almost bewilderingly wide choice of classes, organised by local education authorities and independently run groups all over the country. The Royal School of Needlework and the Embroiderers' Guild (both now established at Hampton Court) attract beginners and experts with a temptingly varied range of subjects. There are summer schools at centres like Missenden Abbey and Gawthorpe Hall. At the latter students can also take advantage of Rachel Kay Shuttleworth's collection, brought together as a source of inspiration and instruction for future generations.

'If you want to be a real embroiderer go to a good course and learn the art', advised Sir David Barran, promoting the City and Guilds Embroidery scheme when, in 1988, an exhibition demonstrating the vigour and diversity of the students' work was held at the Commonwealth Institute in London. As a canvasworker of forty years' experience and a past president of the Embroiderers' Guild, he appreciated the enjoyably challenging nature of this two-part course which covers design, technique, equipment, materials and history. Open to all, it demands a

serious commitment in terms of time and effort, but brings its own reward in the discovery of unsuspected creative energy. Though some who have completed the course might not agree with me, I would say that they have become 'accomplished' in the Elizabethan sense. meaning that they not only *enjoy* but *value* their skill and the sense of achievement it brings.

Some enthusiasts become addicted to courses, learning one technique after another as if to put off the moment of deciding what they really want to do; others become so obsessed with their projects as to remind me of the comments of eighteenth- and nineteenth-century husbands (see pages 61, 68 and 107). Embroidery has always been an agreeably companionable activity, and many husbands, wives and other members of the family work happily together on rugs and other projects today, the radio providing an alternative to someone reading aloud. The number of men, who, like Sir David Barran, enjoy stitching 'at home, in aeroplanes, in cars, anywhere in fact' is increasing all the time. Some brave an otherwise exclusively female class, others develop their ideas on their own. Basil Swindells, an engineer working in physics, now retired, continues to work out mathematical

Bobbydazzler *(1984), a study in triangles by Basil Swindells. Wools re-plyed to increase gradations in colour*

Opposite *Jennifer Wilson's* Passion for Tulips *(1994) reflects contemporary interest in making and stitching on felt, updating its use in eighteenth- and nineteenth-century needlework*

problems in his remarkable series of canvaswork cushions and panels, always starting from a plan on graph paper where permutations of colour can be tried out. Dr Jim Smart's enthusiasm for the plants in his celebrated garden at Marwood Hill in north Devon is carried over into furnishings, such as a rug worked with camellias, grown and bred in the garden, and a wing chair trailed over with clematis. Sir Hardy Amies' love of flowers and devotion to the Winter Queen is similarly recorded in his needlework, which, like Dr Smart's, is an important and regular part of his daily life. Both men use the help of professionals in the drawing out of their designs – a most fruitful collaboration, as we have seen.

The Royal School of Needlework and the Ladies' Work Society (an off-shoot of the School founded by Queen Victoria's artistic daughter, Princess Louise, in 1875 and now established in Moreton-in-Marsh) continue the long established tradition of realising their clients' ideas in well drawn designs, and supplying them with top quality materials. It is here that the manufacturers of kits often fail their customers, offering inferior canvas and dull designs and threads, prettily packaged to promote sales. Though many kits have improved enormously in colourways and design, due in no small measure to Kaffe Fassett's imaginative approach and colour sense and to a growing group of talented designer/embroiderers, there is still truth in the

sad comment made by Ann Macbeth in 1920: 'The British needlewoman follows blindly where the merchant leads.'

We have seen how in the past merchants and manufacturers influenced trends in embroidery with their products. This continues unabated today with the introduction of new materials and computerised machines. Space-dyed and metallic threads and fabric paints and dyes jostle for our attention in specialist shops and at the fairs that have become such a feature of the contemporary scene. Their seductive sparkle and sheen and the spectacular range of colours prove irresistible, but stitched on a multi-coloured, part-sprayed, part-painted ground they can all too easily result in a disastrous over-elaboration of ornament, as unsettling as the worst excesses of Victorian fancy work. The magpie instinct is with us still, and the inadvisability of putting together too many colours, textures and shapes – let alone ideas – is hilariously underlined in A.S. Byatt's wickedly accurate description of a mixed media installation on show in a short story entitled 'Art Work' in *The Matisse Stories* (1993): 'The whole space had been transformed into a kind of soft, even squashy, brilliantly coloured Aladdin's cave. The walls are hung with . . . shifting streams and islands of colour, which when looked at closely reveal little peering mad embroidered faces, green with blue eyes, black with red eyes, pink with silver eyes.'

Opposite Il Rinascimento *(1989), Paddy Killer's self-portrait in drawing, painting and her inimitable machine embroidery celebrates her fortieth birthday*

Paddy Killer illustrates the computer as a design and research tool for the future

Strangely the manufacturers appear quite uninterested in tempting us with tools that are not only a pleasure to use, but to look at as well, which is one reason why, when considering a group of twentieth-century tools to complete the series drawn for this book, Paddy Killer chose to illustrate a computer. While the photocopier, with its invaluable facility for enlarging and reducing motifs to the required size, makes it possible for those who (despite all blandishments) find drawing beyond them to arrive at pleasingly personal designs, the design potential of the computer for domestic embroiderers is as yet little known. The alarm or enthusiasm it excites recalls the argument over machine embroidery earlier in the century, and controversy now, as then, is always a healthy sign. Paddy's witty illustration shows its exciting potential as a tool both for design and research, putting within our reach information about embroidery, tools, materials and so on which might otherwise remain locked away in

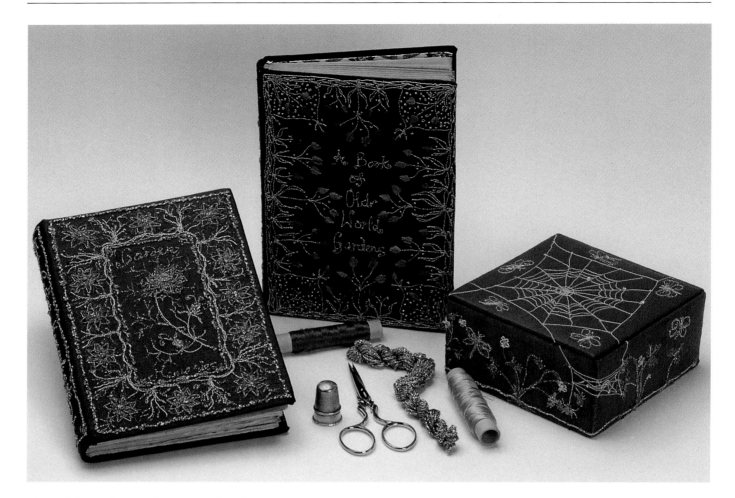

Above *The author's tulip and love-in-a-mist bookcovers and strawberry box were inspired by a bookbinding design by J.T. Cobden-Sanderson and motifs from W. Midgley's* Studies in Plant Form *(1907). They were made for* The Embroiderer's Flowers *exhibition in 1992*

Right *The pattern potential of the computer is demonstrated by Valerie Campbell-Harding in this fractal design altered in a computer paint programme as a design for a small bag (1994). The embroidered fabric, ribbons and threads were stitched to a ground using automatic machine patterns*

museums and libraries. The possibility of seeing on the screen and then selecting, adapting and printing for our own use motifs from rare books, or details from embroideries too fragile to handle, is a thrilling one.

The ornament on the book covers and box on this page was devised from photocopies of motifs by designers and artists whom I particularly admire, and was as pleasurable to think out and adapt as it was to stitch. What I was doing was very little different from the needlewomen who, at the start of this story, chose their motifs from contemporary books and rearranged them to suit their taste. I had not had to prick and pounce the outlines, and I was using a machine for some of the embroidery, yet what I was doing kept bringing to mind the couplet about the Stuart embroiderer who 'her happy hours most happily did spend' in this, for me, the most personal of all the arts.

Bibliography

GENERAL INTEREST

Beck, Thomasina, *Embroidered Gardens,* Angus & Robertson (1979)

    The Embroiderer's Garden, David & Charles (1988)

    The Embroiderer's Flowers, David & Charles (1992)

Brooke, Xanthe, *The Lady Lever Art Gallery Catalogue of Embroideries,* A. Sutton Publishing (1992)

Clabburn, Pamela, *The National Trust Book of Textile Furnishings,* Viking (1988)

    The Needleworker's Dictionary, Macmillan (1976)

Colby, Averil, *Samplers,* Batsford (1964)

Edwards, Joan, *Six Small Books on the History of Embroidery,* Bayford Books (1980-85)

Gardiner, Dorothy, *English Girlhood at School,* Oxford University Press (1929)

Groves, Sylvia, *The History of Needlework Tools and Accessories,* Country Life (1966)

Hackenbrock, Yvonne, *English and Other Needlework, Tapestries and Textiles in the Irwin Untermyer Collection,* Thames and Hudson (1960)

Hughes, Therle, *English Domestic Needlework,* Abbey Fine Arts (1961)

Sebba, Anne, *Samplers: Five Centuries of a Gentle Craft* (1979)

Swain, Margaret, *Historical Needlework,* Barrie and Jenkins (1970)

    Figures on Fabric, A and C Black (1980)

Synge, Lanto, *Antique Needlework,* Blandford Press (1982)

Synge, Lanto, (ed), *The Royal School of Needlework Book of Needlework and Embroidery,* Collins (1986)

THE ELIZABETHAN EMBROIDERER

Arnold, Janet, *The Secrets of Queen Elizabeth's Wardrobe Unlocked,* W. S. Maney (1987)

Ashelford, Jane, *Dress in the Reign of Queen Elizabeth,* Batsford (1988)

Byrne, Muriel St Clare, (ed), *The Elizabethan Home Discovered in Two Dialogues by Peter Erondell and Claudius Hollyband,* Methuen (1949)

Meads, Dorothy, (ed), *The Diary of Lady Margaret Hoby,* Routledge (1930)

Pollock, Linda, *With Faith and Physic, Lady Grace Mildmay, The Life of a Tudor Gentlewoman,* Collins and Brown (1993)

Vernon, Thelma, 'The Inventory of Sir Henry Sherrington' *Wiltshire Archaeological Magazine* (1968)

Wingfield Digby, George, *Elizabethan Embroidery,* Faber (1963)

THE STUART EMBROIDERER

Arthur, Liz, *Embroidery 1600-1700 at the Burrell Collection,* John Murray (1995)

Edwards, Joan, *Crewel Embroidery in England,* Batsford (1973)

Holmes, Martin, *Proud Northern Lady: Lady Anne Clifford, 1590-1676,* Phillimore (1975)

'Selections from the Household Books of Lord William Howard of Naworth Castle' (Surtees Society, 1878)

Swain, Margaret, *Embroidered Stuart Pictures,* Shire (1990)

Yeo, Elspeth and Scott Elliot, A.H., 'Calligraphic Manuscripts of Esther Inglis' *Papers of the Bibliographical Society of America,* Vol 84 (1990)

THE GEORGIAN EMBROIDERER

Day, Angélique, (ed), *Letters from Georgian England. The Correspondence of Mary Delany 1731-68,* The Friar's Bush Press (1991)

Hayden, Ruth, *Mrs Delany: her Life and her Flowers,* Colonnade Books (1980)

Hyde, Mary, *The Thrales of Streatham Park,* Harvard University Press (1977)

Swain, Margaret, *Embroidered Georgian Pictures,* Shire (1994)

REGENCY INTERLUDE

Byrde, Penelope, *A Frivolous Distinction,* Bath City Council (1979)

THE VICTORIAN EMBROIDERER

Callen, Anthea, *Angel in the Studio: Women in the Arts and Crafts Movement,* Astragal (1979)

Levey, Santina, *Discovering Embroidery of the Nineteenth Century,* Shire (1979)

MacCarthy, Fiona, *William Morris: a Life for Our Time,* Faber and Faber (1994)

Marsh, Jan, *Jane and May Morris: A Biographical Story, 1839-1938,* Pandora Press (1986)

Morris, Barbara, *Victorian Embroidery,* Herbert Jenkins (1962)

Parry, Linda, *William Morris Textiles,* Weidenfeld and Nicholson (1983)

Proctor, Molly, *Victorian Canvas Work,* Batsford/Drake (1972)

Uglow, Jenny, *Elizabeth Gaskell: a Habit of Stories,* Faber (1993)

THE TWENTIETH-CENTURY EMBROIDERER

Coss, Melinda, *Bloomsbury Needlepoint,* Ebury Press (1992)

Cumming, Elizabeth, *Phoebe Anna Traquair,* Scottish National Portrait Gallery (1993)

The Embroideress, James Pearsall (1922-39)

Embroidery: The Journal of the Embroiderers' Guild, (1932-94)

Howard, Constance, *Twentieth-Century Embroidery in Great Britain,* 4 Vols, *to 1939, 1940-63, 1964-77, from 1978,* Batsford (1981-6)

Seymour, Miranda, *Ottoline Morrell, Life on the Grand Scale,* Hodder and Stoughton (1992)

The World of Embroidery: The Journal of the Embroiderers' Guild, Neil Hurd (1994 -)

Acknowledgements

Finding the pictures to bring *The Embroiderer's Story* alive presented numerous problems but led to many exciting discoveries and enjoyable meetings. Though readers will find some old favourites, my aim was to introduce as many unfamiliar illustrations as I could in order to demonstrate the amazing variety, beauty and interest of our predecessors' work. I have tried to locate examples undimmed by time, use and light, to show their original appeal. This has been made possible by the museum and gallery curators who have searched through their collections for specific items. It is also the result of the exceptional generosity of the owners of private collections who, while wishing to remain anonymous, have allowed me to photograph their embroideries, fashion plates and book illustrations. Mrs Jean Bowden at the Jane Austen Memorial Trust, Christopher Foley at Lane Fine Art, Stephen and Joy Jarrett and Rebecca Jarrett Scott at Witney Antiques, Constance Howard, Miss Thorold and Stanley Duller at the Ladies' Work Society were kindness itself in helping me. For photography I am greatly indebted to Jim Pascoe, Doctor John Herbert and Christopher Thacker. Paddy Killer and Belinda Downes were a delight to work with, and at David & Charles my editor Vivienne Wells and Cheryl Brown provided much encouragement.

The illustrations are reproduced by kind permission of the following institutions and individuals. Where no credit is given, the illustration is in a private collection, or no longer in copyright.

COLOUR ILLUSTRATIONS

Abbot Hall Art Gallery, 39, 90
Ackworth School, Pontefract, 95 photography by Tony Senior
Agecroft Association, Richmond, Virginia, 41 (top left)
Bishops Stortford Town Council, 149 photography by Gilbert Cox
Bowes Museum, Barnard Castle, Co Durham, 73 (on loan from the Earl of Strathmore), 112
Bridgeman Art Library, 99 (*Mariana in the Moated Grange* [Shakespeare] by Millais, Sir John Everett [1829-96], Private Collection), 105 (*The Lion in Love* by Solomon, Abraham [1824-62], Roy Miles Gallery, 29 Bruton Street, London W1), 116 (*At the Bazaar* or *The Empty Purse* by Collinson, James [1825-81], Sheffield City Art Galleries)
City of Edinburgh Art Collection, 123
City of Rochester upon Medway Guildhall Museum, 93, 101 photography by Dudley Studios
Charleston Trust, 137
Christie's Images, London, 5, 34, 48, 53 (below), 58 (below)
Courtauld Institute of Art, 26
Dorking Embroiderers' Guild, 144
Downes, Belinda, 151 photography by Jim Pascoe
The Embroiderers' Guild Museum Collection, 104
Fiennes, Mark, photography 82
Gibbs, Christopher, 67
The Mistress and Fellows of Girton College, Cambridge, 148
Glasgow Museums and Galleries, The Burrell Collection, 52
Hartnoll, Julian, 128
Holborne Museum, Bath, 134
Hulse, Edward, 55
Jane Austen Memorial Trust, Chawton, Hants, 89 photography by Jim Pascoe
Jarvis, Antony, 54
Killer, Paddy, 154
Ladies' Work Society, 101, 107, 113
Lane Fine Art, 13, 35

Leicester Museums and Galleries, 102
Leeds City Art Gallery, 11
Museum of Costume, Bath 65 (below)
Museum of London, 63
National Galleries of Scotland, 43 (left); 85, 125 photography by Antonia Reeve
National Library of Scotland, 41 (right)
National Portrait Gallery, 106
National Trust, 17 photography by John Bethell; 22 photography by Andrew Haslam; 64 photography by Tynephoto; 74 photography by C. Thacker; 129 photography by Eagle
Newport Museum, Gwent, 70
Nottingham City Museum, 100
Preservation Society of Newport County, Rhode Island, 21
Rijksmuseum, 71
The Royal Collection 1995, Her Majesty the Queen, 76, 79
Ryle-Hodges, Eddie, 80 photography
Society of Antiquaries of London, 117
Trustees of the National Galleries of Scotland, 43 (left), 85, 125
Victoria and Albert Museum, 27; 28 (above), 68, 131 photography by C. Bishop; 114, 127 photography by M. Kitcatt
The Viscount Cowdray, 26 (left) photography by Courtauld Institute of Art
Whitworth Art Gallery, University of Manchester, 7
Witney Antiques, 6, 75, 100

BLACK AND WHITE ILLUSTRATIONS

Birmingham Museums and Art Gallery, 77, 118 (above)
British Library, 8, 26 (below left)
British Museum, 44 (below), 93
Burghley Estates, 91
Campbell-Harding, Valerie, 156
Cutlers Company, 25 photography by John Herbert
Dorking Embroiderers' Guild, 115
Downes, Belinda, 152 (top left) photography by Jim Pascoe
Fitzwilliam Museum, 81
Folger Shakespeare Library, 33 (below right)
Howard, Constance, 145, 89, 90
Killer, Paddy, 24, 39, 82, 94, 154
Lane Fine Art, 14 (top left), 33 (top left)
Leeds City Art Galleries, 72 photography by Courtauld Institute of Art
London Library, 28 (below), 62, 108, 120, 123
The Marquess of Bath, 78 (above)
Metropolitan Museum of Art, 14, 32, 43 (top right), 107
National Maritime Museum, 74 (above)
National Portrait Gallery, 36 (top left)
National Trust, 29; 78 photography by The National Portrait Gallery
Northern Centre for Contemporary Arts, 151 (top right)
Pennington-Mellor-Munthe Trust, 20 (above) photography by Courtauld Institute of Art
Rijksmuseum, 23
Scottish Record Office, 14 (top right)
Victoria and Albert Museum, 19; 21 (below), 28 (centre right) photography by C. Bishop; 30 (below right), 40, 41, 69, 70
Whitworth Art Gallery, University of Manchester, 49
Witney Antiques, 73

PRINTED SOURCES

Huxley, Juliet, *The Leaves of the Tulip Tree,* John Murray Ltd, 138

Belinda Downes' dress accessories were inspired by motifs in Costume Parisien *1817*

Index

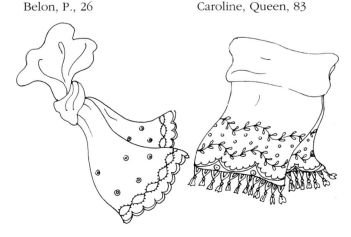